Organ Transplantation, Euthanasia, Cloning and Animal Experimentation

An Islamic View

Abul Fadl Mohsin Ebrahim

THE ISLAMIC FOUNDATION

Published by

THE ISLAMIC FOUNDATION,

Markfield Conference Centre, Ratby Lane,
Markfield, Leicester LE67 9SY, United Kingdom
Tel: (01530) 244944/5, Fax: (01530) 244946
E-mail: i.foundation@islamic-foundation.org.uk
Web site: www.islamic-foundation.org.uk

Quran House, P.O. Box 30611, Nairobi, Kenya

P.M.B. 3193, Kano, Nigeria

British Library Cataloguing in Publication Data

Ebrahim, Abul Fadl Mohsin
Organ transplantation, euthanasia, cloning and animal experimentation : an Islamic view
1. Bioethics – Religious aspects – Islam
2. Islamic ethics
I. Title
297.5'64957

ISBN 0 86037 331 2

Typeset by: N.A. Qaddoura
Cover design by: Imtiaze A. Manjra
Printed in Great Britain by Antony Rowe Ltd.

Dedicated to my teacher

Dr Seyyed Hossein Nasr

University Professor of Islamic Studies,
The George Washington University,
Washington, DC, USA

بسم الله الرحمن الرحيم

CONTENTS

ACKNOWLEDGEMENTS

I am indebted first and last to Almighty Allah ﷻ for having made it possible for me to undertake and complete the writing of this book.

I wish to express my heart-felt gratitude to my teacher Dr Seyyed Hossein Nasr (University Professor of Islamic Studies, The George Washington University, Washington, DC) for guiding my interest and my efforts to the field of bioethics.

My gratitude also goes to Dr Shabbir Wadee (Professor of Forensic Pathology, Tygerberg Hospital, Cape Province, South Africa) for furnishing me with copies of the *fatāwā* (Islamic juridical dicta) that were issued by the South African Islamic religious organizations on the issues discussed in the relevant chapters of this book.

I was encouraged to write this book when I came into contact with three young South African Muslims whose quality of life, by Allah's grace, was enhanced as a result of organ transplantation: the late Sadeck E. Essay (recipient of a donor kidney); Farouk Kara of Durban (recipient of a donor heart); and Goolam Habib Madari who received a donor kidney from his brother Badruddeen.

I thank the Islamic Foundation, Markfield, Leicestershire, UK, for preparing the manuscript and undertaking the publication of this book.

Finally, I express my sincere gratitude to my beloved parents for their unceasing support, love and affection; likewise, to my uncles, aunts, brothers and sisters and wife's family for their good wishes and to my wife and daughters for their patience and understanding during the process of writing this book.

Wa mā tawfīqī illā bi Allāh.

Durban, South Africa,
Rajab 1421/October 2000

Abul Fadl Mohsin Ebrahim

INTRODUCTION

The Qur'ān, in various passages, emphasizes the fact that Allah ﷻ is the One who bestows life and causes to die. For example:

> *It is Allah Who creates you, and takes your souls at death; and of you there are some who are sent back to a feeble age, so that they know nothing after having known (much): For Allah is All-Knowing, All-Powerful.* (al-Naḥl, 16:70)

From this verse we understand that death is inevitable 'in time': it may occur at any time during infancy or youth or old age. The verse alludes to the helplessness of senility that some people experience during their extended life span.[1] It is also the case that before his inevitable end man is afflicted, many a time, with diseases which necessitate his resorting to medical care and attention. Often, he is able to overcome his ailments by resting, by taking relevant medications, by observing an appropriate diet, and so on. However, we cannot rule out the possibility that at some point in life one of his organs may cease to function properly. In this event, depending on the nature of the damage, he may have to undergo corrective surgery or have the defective organ replaced altogether.

I. Organ Transplantation: Its Origin

Replacing diseased or damaged organs is by no means a modern innovation. Jeff E. Zhorne points out that as early as the 8th century BC, Hindu surgeons performed skin transplants to replace noses lost due to syphilis, physical combat, or punishment for crimes.[2]

Likewise, in the *Ḥadīth* literature, there is the incident of ʿUfrajah (May Allah be pleased with him), a *ṣaḥābī* (Companion) of the Prophet Muḥammad ﷺ who lost his nose during a battle and had it replaced with one made out of silver. His silver nose soon gave rise to a bad smell and he sought the advice of the Prophet ﷺ who counselled him to have another one made out of gold.[3] However, transplantation of an organ from the same species was not achieved until 1913 when Dr Alexis Carrel, a French surgeon, succeeded in transplanting a kidney from one cat to another. This became possible only after he had mastered the sewing of severed blood vessels end to end enabling them to carry blood as efficiently as they had before the operation.[4] Thereafter, in the early 1950s, an orthotopic heart transplant in a dog was carried out.

In preparation for the first-ever human heart transplant, Professor Christiaan N. Barnard and his team of surgeons practised orthotopic heart transplants in dogs and performed a kidney transplant on a certain Mrs Black. Subsequently, on 3 December 1967, Barnard and his South African surgical team made history by transplanting the heart of Denise Darvall, a 24-year-old woman, certified brain dead after involvement in a motor vehicle accident, into 54-year-old Louis Washkansky. Washkansky lived for 18 days and died as a result of a lung infection which led to the weakening of the heart from lack of oxygen. About a month later, on 2 January 1968, Barnard performed yet another heart transplant. The recipient of the donor heart was Dr Philip Blaiberg, a Cape Town dental surgeon, who eventually left hospital to return to a full and active life. Commenting on his patient's amazing recovery, Barnard wrote: 'His courage and fortitude did much to establish heart transplantation as a realistic option for future patients with terminal heart disease.'[5]

II. Types of Organ Transplantation

We have made reference above to skin transplants, replacement of organs by artificial ones, kidney transplants in cats, heart transplants in dogs, and kidney and heart transplants in humans. It is essential, if we are to discuss the ethico-legal problems that organ transplantation poses, to indicate clearly the different types of organ transplantation available.

M.F.A. Woodruff identifies at least three types:[6]

A. *Autotransplants*

These are transplants of pieces of tissue or organ from the patient's own body. Transplants of skin, cartilage, tendon and bone are extensively used in orthopaedic surgery.

B. *Homotransplants/Allotransplants*

These involve the transplantation of organs within the same species, one person to another, or from one animal to another of the same species. Some homotransplants/allotransplants do not survive very long. They are nevertheless therapeutically useful since they assist the patient to get over a temporary crisis – for example, in case of blood transfusion, or transplants of bone which provide a form of framework enabling or assisting regeneration of the patient's own tissue. However, not all homotransplants/allotransplants are rapidly destroyed. There are exceptions as in kidney, liver, lung and heart transplantations. Transplant of a tissue which is avascular, like the cornea, is likewise an exception. The success of such transplants depends on the compatibility of donor and recipient tissues. It is a normal procedure, therefore, to establish the degree of compatibility prior to operation in order to lessen the risk of rejection.

C. *Heterotransplants*

These are transplants from animal to man or between animals of different species. Thus far, an unsuccessful attempt was made at California's Lome Linda University Medical Center to replace Baby Fae's defective heart with that of a baboon. Likewise, in England experimental work has begun with the aim of transplanting pigs' kidneys into sheep and eventually into human beings.[7]

III. Scope of the Problem

The primary objectives of organ transplantation are to alleviate suffering and improve quality of life for the patient. Nevertheless it gives rise to a host of ethico-legal issues. Autotransplants do not pose any problem since they are transplants of pieces of tissue or organ from one part of the patient's own body to another. But the other two types of organ transplantation do pose a number of problems:

1. The transplantation of pig kidneys, which are about the same size as human kidneys, is likely to be feasible in the near future and therefore a viable option.[8] It is common knowledge that the *Sharīʿah* (Islamic Law) forbids partaking of the flesh of dead animals and that of the pig. However, in the desperate case of possible starvation or total absence of alternative food, the rule is waived on the basis of necessity in order to preserve human life. Could Muslims therefore accept the kidneys of pigs in the event that theirs fail to function? If the answer is affirmative, it becomes imperative to investigate the legitimacy of animal experimentation from an Islamic viewpoint.
2. Blood transfusion assists a patient to overcome a temporary crisis of loss or lack of blood and is categorized as a form of transplant. Does the *Sharīʿah* sanction it? This question is pertinent in view of the fact that *Fiqh* (Islamic Jurisprudence) regards any form of blood that oozes out of the body as *najas* (impure). If it can be ascertained that the *Sharīʿah* does sanction blood transfusion, would it be *jā'iz* (permissible) to transfuse non-Muslim blood into Muslims and vice versa?
3. Muslims believe that whatever they own has been given to them as an *amānah* (trust) from Allah ﷻ. Would it be a breach of this trust to consent to the removal of parts of the body, when still alive, for the purpose of transplantation in order to enhance the quality of life of another, say one's child, sibling or parent?

4. The *Sharīʿah* emphasizes the sacredness of the human body. Would it be an act of aggression against the human body, tantamount to mutilation, if organs were to be removed after death for the purpose of transplantation?
5. Kidneys for transplantation may be obtained either from living donors or cadavers, while obviously the heart, liver, lung and cornea can be taken from persons who have been certified clinically dead (i.e. when heartbeat and respiration have ceased). However, waiting for the cessation of all vital functions before attempting to obtain the desired organs could result in their being damaged and therefore unfit for transplantation. Could Muslims accept total irreversible loss of cerebral function as a plausible definition of death?
6. Human cloning technology may in future make the regrowing of human parts/organs a reality. Would Muslims be justified in using human cloning for therapeutic purposes?
7. Finally, in view of the fact that organ transplantation cannot resolve the problem of the terminally ill, would euthanasia be a permissible way of ending the suffering of the terminally ill?

These are all pertinent questions which will be taken up in the ensuing discussion. Readers should be aware that the Qur'ān and the *Sunnah* of the Prophet Muḥammad ﷺ neither sanction nor condemn organ transplantation. The discussion in this book is therefore based on the juristic guidelines given on the issues in question. Though these guidelines have been deduced from the broad teachings of the Qur'ān and the *Sunnah*, difference of opinions do exist among the *fuqahā'* (Muslim jurists) on all the issues addressed in this book. This book, of course, is not the final answer to the above-mentioned problems, but, *inshā'Allāh*, it may serve as a starting point for further study of the complexities of these and related issues.

Part One

Animal Experimentation

CHAPTER I

ANIMAL RIGHTS: A HISTORICAL SURVEY

I. Vivisection

The attitudes of humans toward animals are varied. There is a general tendency to be attracted to cuddly creatures and feel aversion to creepy-crawlies. There are some people who consume the flesh of animals, while others choose to be vegetarians. Hunting expeditions are undertaken by some merely as a sport, while others engage in poaching for monetary gains, e.g. the ivory trade.

The term 'vivisection' (derived from the Latin *vivus* and *secare*) literally means to dissect a living animal, but in general modern usage is applied to all types of experiments on living animals (whether or not dissection is involved) for the purpose of obtaining information presumed beneficial to biomedical progress.

Vivisection is not an altogether new procedure. It was reportedly practised by Herophilus about 300 BC,[1] and there is evidence that Galen (129–99), the renowned Greek physician, also made use of vivisection.[2] In the Islamic world, Abū Bakr al-Bayṭār, the Egyptian veterinary surgeon, was the first person to write on the use of animal organs in therapeutics in his celebrated work on veterinary medicine, *Kāmil al-Ṣināʿatayn*.[3]

Today, the popular term for animal experimentation is vivisection. There is little doubt that experiments on invertebrate and vertebrate organisms have contributed immensely to the advancement of medical and surgical practice. The anti-toxin which prevents and cures diptheria was discovered through animal experiments; so too were the anaesthetic properties of ether and chloroform.[4] Brain surgery as it is known today was made possible as a result of experiments carried out on animals which led to the discovery of the localization of control centres in the brain.[5] Likewise, as discussed earlier, in preparation for the first-ever human heart transplant, Barnard and his team of surgeons practised heart transplants in dogs.[6] More generally, since there are important similarities in the body functions of different mammals, modern drugs are tested for side effects on animals before human use.

It must be conceded that, in the absence of legislation to control animal experimentation, animals can be abused in this process. In the 19th century, there was a public outcry in Britain against certain needlessly cruel and frequent experiments on animals. To rectify the situation, a Royal Commission was set up in 1875. In 1876 a law was enacted to control such experiments, permitting experimentation only to licensed persons in special places. Laws regulating vivisection also exist in countries like Italy, Hungary and Poland and others. A law similar to that in Britain was passed in Germany in 1934. In the USA the existing laws on cruelty to animals are considered adequate to cover any abuses in these procedures.[7] In the Islamic world, we find that when the institution of the *khilāfah* (Caliphate) prevailed, it was the duty of the one appointed as the *muḥtasib* (i.e. an inspector who was entrusted to curb any form of malpractice within the society).[8]

II. Animals and Pain

The belief that since animals, unlike humans, are incapable of rational thought or consciousness, they were also incapable of pain except as a form of reflex, prevailed in Europe from the time of Descartes (1596–1650), well into the 19th century. It was used to justify physiological experiments in dogs without the use of anaesthetics.[9] By contrast, the utilitarian philosophy of Jeremy Bentham (1748–1832) contributed towards the realization that animals do suffer pain. He wrote: 'The question is not can they reason? Can they talk? But can they suffer?'[10] This was a significant step in the sense that during the 17th and 18th centuries, sports like bull-baiting, bear-baiting, cock-fighting and cock-throwing (throwing sticks at cocks until they were killed) were widespread in England.[11]

III. Antivivisection Movement

In 1875, Frances Power Cobbe founded the Victoria Street Society in London which, in effect, marked the birth of the antivivisection movement. This society campaigned for the imposition of legal restraints on vivisection. Its members protested in favour of the use of anaesthetics in surgical experiments and for euthanasia (painless death) after experiments. As a result of their efforts, the Cruelty to Animals Bill was passed in 1875. However, this bill had to be amended because scientists felt that permission should be granted for the recovery of animals under some circumstances and the omission of anaesthesia in others. This amendment infuriated Cobbe who then resolved to establish the first explicitly antivivisection society – the Society for the Protection of Animals from Vivisection. Thereafter, other societies came into existence in different parts of the world – the German League Against Scientific Animal Torture in 1879, the Societé Contre la Vivisection in 1882 and the American Anti-Vivisection Society in 1883.[12]

The activities of the antivivisectionists estranged scientists to such an extent that no meaningful dialogue could take place between them. In 1926, Charles Hume took a positive step to remedy the situation by founding the London Animal Society (later the Universities Federation for Animal Welfare (UFAW)) which succeeded in making people think rationally about the suffering of all animals (including pests) so that practical ways of alleviating suffering could be tried. Hume argued that while it might not be possible to ascertain definitely whether or not animals felt pain in the same manner as humans, one could not altogether dismiss the notion that animals feel some sort of pain.[13] There is little doubt that his argument led to the formulation of ethical guidelines for the use of animals in experimentation.

CHAPTER 2

ANIMAL CARE IN ISLAM

I. Human Dominion

The Qur'ān, in various passages, emphasizes the fact that Allah ﷻ has granted human beings dominion over all that exists in the universe. For example:

> *And He has made of service to you whatever is in the heavens and whatever is on the earth; it is all from Him; in that are signs indeed for those who reflect.* (al-Jāthiyah, 45:13)

This verse in no way suggests that human beings have *carte blanche* to do as they please, nor have they any unlimited right to manipulate nature to the extent of disrupting its ecological balance. Likewise, it does not behove them to abuse animals for sport, nor to subject them to indiscriminate experimentation. The underlying significance of the verse is to impress upon them that their Creator has placed all that exists as *amānah* (trust) in their hands.

II. Human Responsibility

The Qur'ān frequently reminds man that he will be held accountable for all his actions, as in this verse:

> *If anyone does a righteous deed, it is to (the benefit of) his soul; if he does evil, it is against (his soul). And then you will all be brought back to your Lord.* (al-Jāthiyah, 45:15)

Human beings should, therefore, make use of all things in a responsible manner. In this regard, Muḥammad Fazlur Raḥmān Anṣārī writes:

All things having been created for our benefit, it becomes our natural duty to:

i. protect everything from damage;
ii. employ it for our benefit in keeping with its dignity as God's creation;
iii. promote its well-being, as far as possible, thereby establishing our thankfulness to God for His blessing in a practical manner.[1]

III. Animals: Their Utility

On the issue of domestic animals, the Qur'ān indicates in *Sūrah al-Naḥl* several ways in which they benefit mankind:

a. *And He has created cattle for you: you get from them your warm garments and other benefits, and of their meat you eat.* (16:5)
b. *And they carry your heavy loads to lands that you could not otherwise reach save with laborious strain to yourselves: for your Lord is indeed Most Kind, Most Merciful.* (16:7)
c. *And He has created horses, mules, and donkeys for you to ride as well as for adornment; and He has created other things of which you have no knowledge.* (16:8)

Let us consider the implications of the verses just cited. In connection with verse (a), we must note that the skins and furs of domesticated animals are permissible for use. However, the Prophet Muḥammad ﷺ prohibited using the skins of wild animals even as floor coverings.[2] If this injunction had been upheld by all, it would have put an end to the senseless killing of certain wild animals for profit. Also, although Muslims are permitted to consume the flesh of certain animals, it must be borne in mind that this does not justify indiscriminate or unrestrained slaughter of them.

In connection with verses (b) and (c), we must remember that Arabs were totally dependent on animals, especially camels, which helped carry their goods for trade to far-off lands. However, the Prophet Muḥammad ﷺ cautioned that the animals in such service should be well-cared for during the journey. For example, he said:

> When you journey through a fertile land, go slowly in order to let your camels graze. When you pass through a barren and dry area, quicken your pace lest hunger should enfeeble the animals...[3]

Likewise, he advised his Companions that even when they had to break their journey to offer *Ṣalāh* (obligatory prayers), they should first unsaddle their animals, meaning that they should unburden the animals and attend to their needs (i.e. feed them).[4]

He ﷺ warned that animals must be made use of for the purpose for which they are meant. Once he saw a man on the back of his camel in a market-place, addressing people. He told him:

> Do not use the backs of your beasts as pulpits, for Allah has made them subject to you so that they take you to places that you could not otherwise reach without bodily fatigue.[5]

Ḥaḍrat ʿAlī, the fourth *khalīfah* in Islam (May Allah be pleased with him), advised the people saying: 'Be kind to pack-animals; do not hurt them; and do not load them more than their ability to bear.'[6]

Thus, it is required of human beings that they reciprocate the service they get from their animals by treating them with kindness and assisting them in fulfiling their needs. We are therefore obliged to interact with animals in a rightful manner for they too have been created by the One Who gave us the gift of life, as the following verse makes clear:

> *There is not an animal on the earth, nor a creature that flies on its wings, but they are communities like you. Nothing have We omitted from the Book. Then they shall all be gathered to their Lord.* (al-Anʿām, 6:38)

IV. Islamic Code of Conduct Towards Animals

It is self-evident that animals do not themselves possess the faculty of demanding their rights from us. Rather, from the Islamic perspective, it is seen as an obligation on us to render animals every kindness and consideration that is their right. Accordingly, in what follows, we shall attempt to construct an Islamic code of conduct towards animals.

A. *Preservation of Life*

The Prophet ﷺ forbade purposeless killing of animals. He said:

> Whoever kills (even) a sparrow or anything smaller, without its deserving it, Allah will question him about it.[7]

Abū Bakr, the first *khalīfah* in Islam (May Allah be pleased with him), heeding the *ḥadīth* just cited, gave the following order to the Muslim army before despatching it to Syria:

> Do not slaughter the sheep or cattle or camels except for purposes of food.[8]

B. *Compassionate Treatment*

In order to inspire people to be merciful, the Prophet ﷺ said:

> The Compassionate One has mercy on those who are merciful. If you show mercy to those who are on earth, He Who is in the heaven will show mercy on you.[9]

Moreover, he taught that our attitude and actions towards animals will, *inter alia*, determine our fate in the Hereafter, as reported in two separate incidents:

i. The Prophet ﷺ told his Companions of a woman who would be sent to Hell for having locked up a cat neither feeding it, nor setting it free so that it could feed itself.[10]
ii. He ﷺ also told them of a man who was blessed by Allah for saving the life of a dog by giving it water to drink and quenching its thirst.[11]

C. *Prohibition of Inciting Animals to Fight*

The Prophet ﷺ prohibited people from engaging in the cruelty of inciting animals against one another.[12] From this it is clear that sports like dog-fighting and cock-fighting are forbidden. By inference, bull and bear-baiting are equally abominable and thus prohibited.

D. *Safety from Target Practice*

It is narrated by Ibn ʿUmar (May Allah be pleased with him) that he came to the house of Yaḥyā ibn Saʿīd while one of Yaḥyā's sons was aiming at a hen after having tied it up. So he walked up to the hen and untied it. Thereafter, he took the boy and the hen to Yaḥyā and told him: 'Prevent your boys from tying this bird with the aim of killing it, for I have heard the Prophet ﷺ forbidding the killing of an animal or other living being after tying them.'[13]

E. *Humane Slaughter*

Muslims are allowed to consume the meat of permissible animals but the Prophet ﷺ cautions them in this regard, saying:

> Allah has prescribed proficiency in all things. Thus if you kill, kill well; and if you perform *dhabḥ* (animal slaughter), perform it well. Let each of you sharpen his blade and let him spare the suffering of the animal he slays.[14]

Moreover, the pronouncement of the *tasmiyah* (uttering the name of Allah) while slaughtering is meant to induce feelings of tenderness and compassion and the prevention of cruelty to animals.

It is thus evident from the teachings of the Qur'ān and the *Sunnah* of the Prophet Muḥammad ﷺ that although man, through Divine Wisdom, has been granted dominion over animals, he has to come to terms with the will of Allah ﷻ that he has moral obligations towards them.

CHAPTER 3

THE PRACTICE OF CLASSICAL MUSLIM PHYSICIANS

Classical Muslim physicians, such as Abū Bakr Muḥammad ibn Zakariyyā al-Rāzī (250–312 AH/865–925) and Abū ʿAlī al-Ḥusayn ibn ʿAbd Allāh ibn Sīnā (370–428 AH/980–1037) and others, were all guided by the Qur'ān and the *Sunnah* of the Prophet Muḥammad ﷺ. For example, in the Qur'ān it is mentioned that the Prophet Ibrāhīm عليه السلام acknowledged that Allah ﷻ is the One Who in reality cured him whenever he fell sick:

> *And when I am ill, it is He who cures me.*
> (al-Shuʿarā', 26:80)

Thus, they, as physicians, regarded themselves as being in service to Allāh ﷻ by extending help to the sick. Moreover, the *Ḥadīth* of the Prophet Muḥammad ﷺ: 'for every ailment there is a cure'[1] prompted them to find cures and remedies which nature provides for the healing of human ills. Futhermore, they were *muttaqīn* (conscious of the presence of Allah ﷻ). This can be deduced from the works of the physician Abū Jaʿfar Muḥammad ibn Abī al-Ashʿath and the Egyptian pharmacist, Abū Munā ibn Abī Naṣr Ḥaffāẓ al-ʿAṭṭār. In his *al-Ghidhā' wa al-Mughtadhī*, Ibn Abī al-Ashʿath warns the physicians against indifference: 'for you will give an account before Allah on what you have done in exercising your profession'.[2] Ibn al-ʿAṭṭār, in his manual on pharmacy entitled *al-Minhāj al-Dukkān fī Ta'rīkh al-Adwiyah al-Nāfiʿah li al-Abdān*, advises his son, as also a pharmacist, and other practising pharmacists to: have deep religious convictions, consideration of others, a sense of responsibility, and be careful and God-fearing.[3]

I. Study of Animals

The first comprehensive book on animals in Arabic was undertaken by Abū ʿUthmān ʿAmr ibn Baḥr al-Jāḥiẓ (d. 255 AH/869) under the title *al-Ḥayawān*. In this work, he described the different kinds of animals that abounded in Iraq and neighbouring countries. He also discussed their characteristics and behaviour, and touched upon their diseases and treatment.

The Egyptian philosopher/theologian Kamāl al-Dīn al-Damīrī (d. 808AH/1406), in his *Ḥayāt al-Ḥayawān* (The Life of Animals), discussed the medicinal value of animal organs which were used in folk medicine.

Abū Bakr al-Bayṭār (d. 740 AH/1340), the Egyptian veterinary surgeon, in his comprehensive work on veterinary medicine *Kāmil al-Ṣināʿatayn*, also dealt with making use of animal organs in therapeutics.[4]

II. Compounded Medications

Abū Bakr Muḥammad ibn Zakariyyā al-Rāzī (Latinized as Rhazes) of Persia, was regarded as the Arab Galen and the unchallenged chief physician of the Muslims. Among his contributions was the introduction of mercury compounds as purgatives. It should be noted that he treated monkeys with these compounds before prescribing them to his patients.[5]

Abū al-Qāsim Khalaf bin ʿAbbās al-Zahrāwī (Latinized as Albucasis) of Andalusia (324–403 AH/936–1013), the famous surgeon, wrote *al-Tasrīf li-man ʿAjiza ʿan al-Ta'līf*, a medical encyclopaedia comprising thirty treatises. The nineteenth treatise is devoted to cosmetology, the art of beautification. In it, compounds made of animal tissues, soft scented dellium, almond and olive oil, etc. are recommeded as remedies for softening the skin of women's hands and wrists.[6] The twenty-eighth treatise deals with the methods of preparing, using, and storing drugs of animal origin, e.g. burning of eggs and sea shells, cooking of snakes and scorpions, bleaching of wax, collecting animal blood and drying animal gall bladders for use in eye treatments.[7]

Abū al-Rayḥān Muḥammad ibn Aḥmad al-Bīrūnī al-Khawārizmī (362–442 AH/973–1051), the father of Islamic pharmacy and marine biology, wrote a book on pharmacy and *materia medica*, namely, *al-Ṣaydanah*. This work is divided into two sections. In its second section, similes' of animal origin are discussed. For example, mention is made of the therapeutic value of the meat of Nicolar or rock-dove, a land animal, to help build blood in anaemic people.[8]

The science of toxicology was given particular coverage in the writings of classical Muslim physicians because there always existed the danger of Muslim rulers and the rich being poisoned by envious enemies.[9] Thus these physicians would test the effectiveness of a theriatic (i.e. a remedy against poisons) by giving a toxic dose of poisonous drug to a rooster, a dog, or other animal and thereafter administering the theriatic to see whether it was effective.[10]

III. Dissection of Animals

Dr Hassan Hathout, former Professor of Obstetrics and Gynaecology, Faculty of Medicine, Kuwait University, points out that anatomy and physiology gained prominence because from these two sciences the signs (*āyāt*) of God in the creation of man can be appreciated. However, he mentions that anatomy was restricted to the dissection of apes since Islamic Law ensured the right of the dead to be properly buried.[11] He may be right in holding this view. The famous Islamic surgeon, al-Zahrāwī, emphasized the need for and value of teaching anatomy and training in surgery but did not indicate in his *al-Tasrīf* whether he dissected human bodies or not.[12]

ʿAlāʾ al-Dīn ʿAlī ibn Abī Ḥazm al-Qurashī (606–686 AH/1210–1288), popularly known as Ibn al-Nafīs, the one who discovered pulmonary circulation, makes it clear, in the introduction of his commentary on Ibn Sīnā's *al-Qānūn*, *Sharḥ al-Qānūn*, that he, for reasons of religion and conscience did not attempt to dissect human bodies.[13]

It may be appropriate to mention here that al-Zahrāwī was the first to use rubbed down and smoothed clean animal gut in wound surgery.[14] In the field of dentistry, he discussed the carving of false teeth from animal bones.[15]

It is therefore apparent that classical Muslim physicians did in fact engage in some form of animal experimentation. In the following chapter, the Islamic legal implication of such experimentation is discussed.

CHAPTER 4

ISLAMIC JURIDICAL PRINCIPLES

The *Sharīʿah* does not deal directly with the issue of animal experimentation *per se*. Likewise, it neither sanctions utilizing of animal tissues and organs for transplantation into humans, nor prohibits it. Islamic jurisprudence is the science which guides Muslims in determining which human decisions in relation to contemporary issues are permissible or not.

I. Animal Experimentation

Islamic jurisprudence takes into consideration the interests (*maṣāliḥ*) of mankind, which are fivefold: religion (*al-dīn*), life (*al-nafs*), family (*al-nasl*), reason/sanity (*al-ʿaql*) and property (*al-māl*).[1] In other words, certain acts motivated by necessity (*al-ḍarūrah*) in order to protect any of these interests may be justified conditionally. In the same manner it may be argued that if animal experimentation is carried out with the aim of gaining knowledge that would prove beneficial to the preservation of human and animal life, then such experimentation could be sanctioned. However, what is termed as a necessary (human) interest (*al-maṣlaḥah al-ḍarūriyyah*) is further restricted by certain broad juristic principles as enumerated below:

i. What leads toward the forbidden, is itself forbidden.[2]
ii. Should one be compelled to choose between two harms ('evils'), opt for the lesser in order to prevent the greater injury.[3]
iii. Whatever is made permissible for a particular reason becomes impermissible once the reason for its permissibility is no longer present.[4]

iv. Resort to alternatives for something in the event of there being no (juristic) justification for that thing.[5]

Therefore, in applying the above juristic principles to animal experimentation the following inferences may be made: Rule (i) would make the subjecting of animals to painful experiments and others that could result in blinding or maiming them as forbidden (*ḥarām*). Rule (ii) would make permissible the testing of certain life-saving drugs upon animals before being declared safe for human use. Rule (iii) would make the subjection of animals to indiscriminate/unecessary experimentation impermissible. Rule (iv) is relevant to the current search for alternatives to experimentation on animals in order to minimize their utilization in experiments.

A. *Ḥalāl (pure and wholesome) Animals to Human Transplants*

Research aimed toward the safe transplantation of animal tissues and organs into humans is currently being conducted in countries like the USA and Great Britain. Would such procedures not be tantamount to tampering with the Divine patterns *(Sunan* of Allah ﷻ) in creation? After all, the Qur'ān refers to Satan's determination to deter man from the Right Path, saying:

> *I (Satan) will mislead them, human beings, and I will arouse desires in them false desires; I will command them and they will slit the ears of cattle, and I will command them and they will change the fair creation of Allah.* (al-Nisā', 4:119)

This dilemma may be answered by arguing that the intention or aim of transplanting animal tissues or organs into humans is undertaken solely for the purpose of saving human life and certainly not for the motive of mutilating the creation of Allah ﷻ. Although the Qur'ān does not touch on the issue of animal to human transplants, it lays the greatest emphasis on saving human life:

> *If anyone saves a life, it shall be as if he has saved the lives of all mankind.* (al-Mā'idah, 5:32)

It is that emphasis that has prompted Muslim jurists to infer that it may be permissible to transplant animal organs into humans. Hence, the following positive juridical rulings:

The Islamic Fiqh Academy of the Muslim World League, Makkah, Saudi Arabia, at its eighth working session which took place from 28 *Rabīʿ* II to 7 *Jumādā* I (19–28 January 1985), resolved that the *Sharīʿah* sanctions the retrieval of animal organs from *ḥalāl* (pure and wholesome) animals which have been slaughtered according to Islamic rites for transplantation into humans.[6]

The Islamic Fiqh Academy of India at its first seminar held in Delhi, India, in March 1989, resolved that it is lawful to replace human organs with that of *ḥalāl* animals, slaughtered according to Islamic rites.[7]

The late Shaykh Jād al-Ḥaqq ʿAlī Jād al-Ḥaqq, the former rector of Al-Azhar University, states in his *Buḥūth wa Fatāwā Islāmiyyah fī Qaḍāyā Muʿāṣarah* (Studies and Islamic Legal Decrees on Modern Problems) that it is permissible to replace the fallen human tooth with that of a pure and wholesome animal.[8]

Dr Fayṣal Ibrāhīm Ẓāhir, Chairman of the Department of Islamic Medicine, King Fayṣal ibn ʿAbd al-ʿAzīz University, Saudi Arabia, in his book *Ḥiwār Maʿ Ṭabīb Muslim* (Dialogue with a Muslim Doctor) states that there is no prohibition on the transplantation of animal organs (retrieved from pure and wholesome animals) into humans for the purpose of saving lives or to improve the quality of the lives of the recipients. He goes on to explain that Allah ﷻ has made these animals subservient to humans.[9]

The Majlis al-ʿUlamā'of Port Elizabeth, South Africa, in response to the questionnaire of the Islamic Medical Association of South Africa regarding animal to human transplants stated that:[10]

It is permissible according to the *Sharīʿah* to transplant animal organs into humans to save a life or to improve the quality of life. This permissibility is based on the following conditions:

a. The organs must be only that of *ḥalāl* animals, i.e. such animals the consumption of which is *ḥalāl* for Muslims, e.g. sheep, goats, cows, etc.

b. The *ḥalāl* animals from which the organs are acquired must be Islamically slaughtered, i.e. *dhabḥ* must be effected.

B. *Pig to Human Transplants*

Muslim jurists differ on the issue of utilizing pig tissues and organs on medical grounds. Some of them regard medicine as not belonging within the same category as that of a compelling necessity like food.[11] In support of their stand, they cite the following *ḥadīth*:

> Assuredly Allah did not provide a cure for you in what He has prohibited for you.[12]

The Majlis al-ʿUlamāʾ of Port Elizabeth take the view that since the pig and all its parts are considered to be grossly impure (*najāsat al-ghalīẓah*) according to the *Sharīʿah*, it is therefore forbidden (*ḥarām*) to derive any benefit from them even if it be on medical grounds or whatever.[13]

On the other hand, there are Muslim jurists who equate medical necessity with that of food since both are crucial to the preservation of life.[14] The Qurʾān permits Muslims, compelled by hunger, to consume the flesh of swine:

> *But if one is forced by necessity, without craving (i.e. wilfully for indulgence's sake), nor transgressing due limits, then no sin shall be upon him for Allah is Oft-forgiving, Most Merciful.* (al-Baqarah, 2:173)

Therefore, the utilization of pig tissues or organs for the sake of saving human life is permissible. In what follows are some of the views of Muslim scholars who subcribe to the view that it is permissible to transplant pig organs into humans on the ground of necessity (*ḍarūrah*), i.e. to save human life:

The Islamic Fiqh Academy of the Muslim World League, Makkah, Saudi Arabia, holds that it is permissible to transplant organs of other animals (i.e. whose meat may not be consumed by Muslims) into humans on the basis of urgent necessity.[15]

The Islamic Fiqh Academy of India also sanctions the retrieval of organs from such animals whose meat is forbidden for Muslims to consume, or from such animals whose meat is wholesome and pure but have not been slaughtered according to Islamic rites for transplantation into humans. However, this permissibility is hedged by two conditions, firstly that there is no alternative procedure available and secondly that the life of the recipient is in jeopardy or his/her organ is in danger of being irreversibly damaged.[16]

Insofar as an organ retrieved from a pig is concerned, Dr Fayṣal Ibrāhīm Ẓāhir is of the view that it is permissible to use it for transplantation into a human being on the basis of the Islamic juridical principle of necessity which renders the forbidden permissible. Permissibility in this case is thus conditional in view of the non-availability of any wholesome (*ḥalāl*) substitute.[17]

Part Two

Blood Transfusion

CHAPTER 5

CONCEPTIONS ABOUT BLOOD

I. In Some Cultures

Blood has, in various cultures and traditions, been viewed differently. For example, the ancient Egyptians annointed their heads with oil and blood as treatment for greying and baldness. The Romans drank blood of the dying gladiators to imbue them with courage.[1] In the pre-Islamic era it was maintained that someone suffering from rabies could be cured by drinking the blood of the chief of the tribe.[2] Some nations even considered drinking the blood of a beheaded criminal to be a remedy. In recent times, there have been reports that certain Central Australian tribes made their sick old men drink the blood of their young men.[3]

In contrast to the above-mentioned beliefs in the curative power of blood, the Bantu tribe in South Africa has the belief that blood that is taken away cannot be reconstituted thus resulting in one's becoming weak, impotent and blind for life.[4]

II. In Certain Religions

The religious traditions like Judaism, Christianity and Islam have viewed blood in a different manner altogether. In the case of Judaism, for example, blood signifies the renewal of the covenant.

The Old Testament tells us that the power of the sacrificial blood is atoning (*Lev.* 16:6, 15ff.), purifying (*Lev.* 14) and sanctifying (*Exo.* 29:30f.). In other words, it is related to the making of the covenant. Therefore, in sacrifices of purification, sin and guilt, the sacrificial blood *ipso facto* removed sin, especially on the great Day of Atonement (*Lev*. 16).[5] However, consuming such blood is forbidden (*Lev*. 3:17).

In Christian theology tremendous importance is given to the blood of Christ (*Heb*. 9:27). The sacrificial blood of Christ has the power to bring forgiveness and sanctification. Moreover, it establishes peace with God and is regarded as the foundation of the new fellowship with God. It ought to be pointed out here that the New Testament also uses the expression 'flesh and blood' in order to denote man's weakness and transitoriness, i.e. his slavery to sin and death.[6]

Islamic jurisprudence categorizes any form of blood that flows out of the body as *najas* (impure).[7] In the instance, therefore, of bleeding resulting from a cut or wound, the worshipper's state of ablution (*wuḍū'*) becomes nullified.[8] So also menstrual bleeding renders a woman ritually unclean. The Qur'ān states (2:222) that the husband must refrain from sexual intercourse with his wife from the beginning until the cessation of her menstruation and until she has purified herself by undertaking the ritual bath (*ghusl*). Likewise, being in the state of menstruation, she may not participate in the obligatory acts of worship.[9]

Moreover, Islam censures its followers from consuming blood. Amongst the *ḥarām* (unlawful) categories of consumable foods mentioned in the Qur'ān is *dam masfūḥ* (lit. blood poured forth):

> *Say (O Muḥammad): 'I do not find in what is revealed to me any thing forbidden to be eaten by one who wishes to eat it, unless it be dead meat, or blood poured forth, or the flesh of swine...'* (al-Anʿām, 6:145)

It may be appropriate to mention here that during the pre-Islamic era a hungry person used to jab a bone or sharp object into the flesh of his animal, then collect and drink its flowing blood. This was an evil practice since it was injurious to the animal and in reality weakened it. However, this is still a common practice of the nomadic pagan tribes of southern Sudan; nomads feed on blood and milk mixed together when travelling with their herds.

Yūsuf al-Qaraḍāwī, in explaining the likely reasons for this prohibition, states that drinking blood may be injurious to health and, moreover, repugnant to human decency.[10] The ultimate wisdom for its prohibition may not be fully realized, but as it is unlawful (*ḥarām*) to consume it, then blood is necessarily placed within the category of impurity (*najas*).

CHAPTER 6

THE REALITY OF BLOOD TRANSFUSION

I. Brief History

Blood transfusion is in effect the injection of blood from one person (called the donor) into the circulatory system of another person (called the recipient). Blood transfusion would not have been possible but for the discovery that there is uninterrupted blood circulation within the body. It is therefore imperative that an account be given of how blood transfusion finally came to be accomplished.

In 1665 Dr Richard Lower, the British anatomist, succeeded in transfusing blood from one dog to another. Two years later, Jean Baptiste Denis, a French doctor, philosopher and astronomist, attempted the first recorded blood transfusion on a human being. He transfused the blood of a lamb into a 15-year-old patient of his. The outcome was disastrous, resulting in the boy's death and charges of murder were laid against him.[1] Thereafter, a long period of stagnation in the applied field of blood transfusion ensued. Some 150 years later, in 1818, Dr James Blundell of St. Thomas's and Guy's Hospitals successfully carried out the first human-to-human blood transfusion. He achieved this only after he had invented an apparatus for directly transfusing blood and he cautioned that only human blood should be transfused in humans. But, the general use of the apparatus invented by Dr Lower was made possible only in 1901. It was then that Karl Landsteiner, a Viennese scientist, discovered that there were different kinds of blood. Thus, if the wrong kinds of blood were mixed, clumping together (agglutination) of red cells would take place, leading to their destruction.[2] At this juncture, therefore, it may be appropriate to briefly discuss the different blood groups, factors which are present in each group, and which groups can be mixed without clumping.

II. Blood Groups[3]

There are four main blood groups: A, B, AB, and O. These groups differ in the presence or absence of two chemical substances (A and B) in the red cells and in the presence or absence of two factors (anti-A and anti-B) in the serum. It ought to be noted that though the serum and the plasma are similar, the difference between them is that in the serum, fibrinogen and much of the other clotting factors are absent. Thus the serum itself cannot clot because of lack of these factors, which are otherwise present in the plasma.[4]

A person who is of blood group O is known as a universal donor in view of the fact that this person's red cells contain neither the chemical substance A nor B. But, such a person may not receive blood from anyone but another of the same O group since his/her serum contains both Anti-A and Anti-B factors. On the other hand, a person with the group AB can receive blood transfusion from any donor and is called a universal recipient, but can donate blood only to another person of blood group AB.[5]

III. Indications for Transfusion

There are basically two general reasons which may necessitate blood transfusion, namely, (a) loss of blood and (b) lack of vital elements in the blood.

A. *Loss of Blood*

Loss of blood may result in reducing the volume of circulating blood and this may be precipitated by the following factors:[6]

i. Haemorrhages caused by wounds, or in ulcer and gastrointestinal cases, or in childbirth.

ii. Injuries, burns and scalds sustained in accidents.

iii. Operative surgery as in the case of cardiovascular surgery and other operations.

iv. Incompatibility of blood between the mother and child. In such cases, exchange transfusions have to be undertaken to save the life of the child.

v. Anaemia, acute and chronic, as well as coagulation disorders such as haemophilia.

B. *Lack of Vital Elements*

A patient may sometimes not require the transfusion of whole blood but, rather, only certain of its vital elements as in the following cases:[7]

i. An anaemic patient who is suffering from lack of red cells may thus require the transfusion of red cells only.

ii. A haemophiliac patient, as a result of a congenital disorder, risks anaemia and dangerous loss of blood should he/she sustain any wound or injury, no matter how minor, because his/her blood tends to clot very slowly. Therefore, in order to arrest bleeding or haemorrhaging, he/she would require transfusion of blood plasma. Alternatively, the patient may be injected with concentrated preparations of AHF (i.e. anti-haemophilic factor).

It ought to be noted here that since plasma is devoid of blood corpuscles, a patient suffering from serious haemorrhage needs at least a pint of whole blood for about every pint of plasma transfused.[8] It may also be necessary to add that before accepting blood from potential donors it is necessary to screen them for diseases such as hepatitis, malaria, syphilis and acquired immunity deficiency syndrome (AIDS) in view of the fact that these diseases can be transmitted by transfusion.

CHAPTER 7

JURISTIC RULINGS

The Qur'ān and the *Sunnah* are silent on the issue of blood transfusion. Blood that is shed (*dam masfūḥ*), however, from the broad principles and general teachings of the original sources of Islam, has always been regarded as impure. It is for this reason that initially blood transfusion posed a genuine problem to the Muslim jurists.

In this chapter an attempt is made to discuss the deliberations of some Muslim scholars on the issue of blood transfusion in order to understand the Islamic approach to the issue in question.

I. Objections to Blood Transfusion

It is the viewpoint of the late Muftī Shafī' of Pakistan that, in ordinary circumstances, blood transfusion is to be regarded as *ḥarām* (forbidden) on the grounds that firstly, blood constitutes part and parcel of the human body and secondly, it falls under the category of *najas* (impurity).[1]

A. *Blood a Part of the Human Body*

Muftī Shafī' argues that since blood is part and parcel of the human body, its extraction and transfusion into someone else's circulatory system would be tantamount to tampering with the honour/dignity of man, hence its prohibition.

B. *Blood as* Najas

Futhermore, Muftī Shafī' points out that extracted blood is intrinsically impure and this he gathers from Imām al-Shāfi'ī's celebrated *Kitāb al-Umm.* Imām Shāfi'ī states:

> If someone inserts blood into his skin and it grows on it (*nabata ʿalayhi*) it becomes compulsory for him to draw out this blood and repeat every *ṣalāh* (prescribed prayer) that he has performed after the said insertion.[2]

II. Relaxation of the Legal Rule

However, it is the verdict of Muftī Shafīʿ that considering the concessions and facilities endowed by the *Sharīʿah* in the event of extraordinary circumstances (i.e. life-threatening situations) and treatment, blood transfusion is *jā'iz* (permissible).[3] In order to lend support to his stance that it is permissible to carry out blood transfusion in extraordinary circumstances, he draws an analogy between milk and blood. Milk, he points out, issues out naturally (when the infant suckles the breast of its mother) and having been part and parcel of the mother's body, it serves as nourishment for the infant once it has thus been consumed. The *Sharīʿah*, he notes, recognizes the invaluable nature of breast milk as nourishment for the infant and has therefore made it an obligation upon the mother to breastfeed her infant in normal circumstances. Muftī Shafīʿ points out that as far as blood is concerned, it is extracted by means of a needle, without resort to the cutting up of any human organ, and transfused into someone else for the purpose of sustaining life.[4] Moreover, he states that the *fuqahā'* have also declared that it is permissible for male adults to make use of breast milk as a form of medicine and for treatment purposes. In this regard, the following statement is found in *Fatāwā ʿĀlamgīriyyaḥ*:

> There is no objection if a man is made to snuff the milk of a woman and drink it (for treatment purposes).[5]

Likewise, Muftī Shafīʿ holds the view that although blood is impure, to donate it in order that it may be transfused into someone else is *jā'iz* (permissible) on the grounds of necessity and falls within the category of making use of forbidden objects as medicine.[6] This permissibility, he cautions, ought to be hedged with the following restrictions:[7]

1. Blood transfusion is permissible in case there is an acute need for it. In other words, there is apprehension on the part of a competent doctor that the patient might lose his/her life, and there is no way of saving the life of the said patient except by recourse to blood transfusion.
2. Blood transfusion is also permissible even when there exists no danger to the life of the patient but, in the opinion of the said doctor, the patient's recovery would not be possible without transfusion.
3. If it is possible to refrain from blood transfusion it is better to do so. For example should there be a conflicting opinion in regard to the question of the patient's recovery then it would be better to avoid transfusion.
4. Blood transfusion is not permissible if its purpose is merely to enhance (health) or to beautify. In other words, no fear exists that the patient's illness would be prolonged, the purpose of the transfusion would be merely to strengthen the body or to increase its beauty.

III. Justifications for Blood Transfusion

Shaykh Aḥmad Fahmī Abū Sinnah, member of the Islamic Fiqh Academy of the Muslim World League, Makkah, Saudi Arabia, argues against objections to blood transfusion as follows:[8]

A. *The Dignity of Man*

The extraction of blood from the donor and its transfusion into the recipient does not in any way tamper with human honour/dignity. Rather, such an action enhances human honour/dignity since it is a very humane gesture of assistance to a fellow human being, even to the end of helping save his/her life. Moreover, this action may be regarded as a *jihād* should it be effected for the benefit of the *mujāhidīn* (who have sustained heavy injuries on the battlefield).[9]

B. *The Rule of Necessity*

Blood transfusion is permissible in view of the fact that there does not exist any stipulation against it in the original sources of Islam. The only references made to blood *per se* are those pertaining to its impurity and the prohibition of consuming it. But these restrictions will not apply in times of acute necessity when transfusion is the only means of saving life as is the case of relaxation of the Law regarding forbidden foods, in order to sustain life.

Moreover, man's right over his blood is waived in the event of his consenting to donate it. However, Islamic Law may intervene in such situations where the life and health of the donor is affected in any way through his donating blood. Thus, the following conditions must be fulfilled:[10]

1. The donor has willingly consented to donate his blood.
2. No grave danger to his life or health exists through the transfusion. This can be ascertained by a competent and trustworthy doctor.
3. It must be established that there is no other way of saving the life of the blood recipient except by transfusion of blood.
4. The degree of the success through this treatment is anticipated as high.

As far as storing blood, (e.g. in blood banks) for possible transfusion into those who sustain injuries as a result of war, factory and motor vehicle accidents, Shaykh Abū Sinnah is of the view that it is permissible to take such a precautionary measure in order to ascertain the availablity of blood in times of need.[11]

C. *Human Welfare*

Dr ʿAbd al-Salām al-Shukrī Professor of *Sharīʿah* and Law, Al-Azhar University, Egypt, is of the view that blood transfusion is a permissible procedure since it is aimed at averting a tangible danger to the life of the recipient. However, he is of the view that its permissibility is conditional on the following grounds:[12]

1. That the donor should not demand any form of financial reward for his service. [13]
2. That the donor's life should in no way be placed in danger as a result of the extraction of blood from him/her.
3. That the donor should be free from any form of infectious/ contagious diseases and not hooked on any form of addiction.[14]

D. *Blood Transfusion: A Form of Cure*

The late Shaykh Jād al-Ḥaqq ʿAlī Jād al-Ḥaqq states that it is permissible within the *Sharīʿah* to derive benefit from a part of the human body such as blood, for example, and to transfuse it into another person as a form of treatment in the event that there exists no other form of cure.[15]

Similarly, Shaykh Mannāʿ ibn Khalīl al-Qaṭṭān, Professor at the University of Muḥammad ibn Saʿūd, Riyadh, Saudi Arabia, holds the view that blood transfusion is a form of treatment. He points out that it would be permissible to donate blood if the intention is to store it in order to make use of it in the hour of need but it would be mandatory to do so in order to save the life of another person.[16]

Shaykh Ḥasanayn Muḥammad Makhlūf, the former Grand Muftī of Egypt, in his *Fatāwā Sharīʿah* also ratifies transfusing blood into a patient on the advice of the attending physician who is of the opinion that this procedure is necessary in order to save his/ her life.[17]

IV. The Donor

Richard M. Titmuss a pioneer in the field of blood transfusion research identifies eight types of donors. He correctly suggests that these donors 'ought to be referred to as suppliers' in view of the fact that their 'donating' blood is not altruistically motivated.[18]

The following summary of each type of donor will undoubtedly lend support to this view:[19]

A. *The Paid Donor*

The primary motive of this donor is limited to the selling of his blood at the market price. He/she undertakes this exercise simply as an alternative means of acquiring wealth.

B. *The Professional Donor*

This donor is a registered donor and gives blood more or less on a regular basis. Besides being paid, on a weekly or monthly basis, this donor may also be compensated with daily supplements of iron.

C. *The Paid and Induced Donor*

This type of donor is given payment for the service rendered. His donating blood is not a spontaneous action but he is induced to do so under group pressure at his work-place or within society.

D. *The Responsibility Fee Donor*

This donor is one who has received blood transfusion and is required to repay the service in blood or money. In other words, such a donor is one who is impelled, owing to recovery from prior sickness, to donate blood. For every unit of blood received this donor is required to replace two to three units in its place.

E. *The Family Credit Donor*

This type of donor makes an advance donation of one pint of blood each year so as to assure in return his and his family's future blood requirements.

F. *The Captive Voluntary Donor*

This type includes members of the Defence Forces and prison inmates. Members of the Defence Forces are usually urged to volunteer their blood. In return for this service, they are paid and may also enjoy other benefits, such as additional leave. Prison inmates are also paid for their blood and at times may even benefit by remission of their respective sentences.

G. *The Fringe Benefit Voluntary Donor*

This donor's incentive is motivated by the fringe benefits offered by the State. Some of the fringe benefits include days off on full pay and free holidays.

H. *The Voluntary Community Donor*

This type of donor may be regarded as the only genuine donor, for this donor is prepared to donate blood freely to anyone whether named or unnamed. The donor's motivation is simply altruism towards the community at large.

Analyzing these categories of donors within the Islamic system the following may be observed:

i. Categories A, B, C and F would be unacceptable on the basis of their being a form of blood 'trafficking' (see[13] above).
ii. Categories E and H could be regarded as acceptable in that their motivation is anticipation of times of acute need when blood would be necessary. For example, in times of war (see[9] above). However, it ought to be reiterated here that, within the parameters of Islamic jurisprudence, donating one's blood is governed by certain conditions which need to be fulfilled by potential donors (see[14] above).
iii. Category G may not pose a problem to Shaykh Abū Sinnah in view of the fact that he is of the opinion that there is no objection to the State's encouraging people to donate blood by paying them money to buy foodstuff in order to replenish their lost energies.[20] Likewise, according to the decision of the Islamic Fiqh Academy of the Muslim World League, Makkah, Saudi Arabia, there is no prohibition on encouraging the blood donor by giving him/her money as a donation or reward for providing this humane service.[21]

V. Sale of Blood

Muslim scholars are in agreement that it is not permissible to indulge in the sale of blood. Here, it may be appropriate to reiterate that according to Islamic Law, blood that flows out of the body is considered to be impure and this is deduced from the Qur'ānic verse:

> *He has forbidden to you only dead meat, and blood, and the flesh of swine...* (al-Baqarah, 2:173)

According to the principles of Islamic Law, if something has been forbidden to Muslims, the buying and selling of it is also prohibited.[22] Thus Abū Sinnah maintains that the selling of blood is not permissible on two counts, its impurity and the potential harm that it may lead to. Greed for money may cause one to place one's life in danger if one were to have too much of one's blood extracted.[23]

At this juncture, further light may be shed on the prohibition of the sale of blood on the basis of the following *ḥadīth*:

> The Prophet ﷺ prohibited taking money for blood, the price of a dog, and the earnings of a slave-girl by prostitution. He cursed the one who tattoos and the one who gets tattooed, the eater of *ribā* (usury) and the maker of pictures.[24]

Muslim jurists, while deliberating on the issue of the sale of blood, try to establish the *ʿillah* (effective reason) for such a prohibition. In other words, they conclude that it is forbidden to sell blood on the ground that the above-mentioned Qur'ānic verse prohibits Muslims from consuming blood and the above *ḥadīth* prohibits Muslims from selling that which is termed as prohibited. Thus the effective reason for the prohibition of the sale of blood is its inherent impure nature.[25]

Muftī Shafīʿ concurs that the sale of blood is impermissible (*ghayr jā'iz*). However, he points out that in times of acute need, it is permissible to pay a price in order to obtain blood on condition that the blood cannot be procured otherwise, i.e. free of charge.

He adds that it is improper for the donor to stipulate a fee for his blood.[26]

The sale of an intrinsically unclean object is not permissible on account of its being contemptible. The use of such an object (swine bristles, for example) as lace is permissible in case of necessity since something else may not perform its function. It may be argued that if this is so then it is obligatory that its sale be rendered permissible. In answer to that it ought to be said that should the permissible object be found then there would be no necessity for its sale. Consequently, it may be argued that if it cannot be acquired except by purchase then it would be permissible. However, the seller may not stipulate a price. The jurist Abū al-Layth says that if the shoemakers cannot find swine bristles except by purchase, it is permissible for them to do just that, i.e. purchase it.[27]

Likewise, it is to be noted that the Islamic Fiqh Academy of the Muslim World League, Makkah, during its 11th meeting (19–26 February 1989) ratified that there is no prohibition if a person, compelled by necessity (i.e. if there is no other means to obtain blood except by paying for it), pays the stipulated fee in order to receive blood transfusion. Thus, the one who pays for the service is absolved from any misconduct (guilt), while it is the one who accepts payment for this service who actually sins.[28]

VI. Blood Banks

Notwithstanding the fact that considerable research is being made in the field of medical science to find a substitute for human blood, there is an ongoing demand for blood in both the technologically advanced countries and in the underdeveloped ones. In order, therefore, to create an awareness of the need and urgency to ensure the continuous availability of blood, it is imperative that an estimate be given as to the amount of blood required in certain medical procedures:[29]

i. victims of serious accidents may require transfusion of 20 pints of blood or more.

ii. 20 pints or more of blood may also be required by a maternity patient as a result of blood loss after childbirth.
iii. 12 to 15 pints of blood are required to prime the heart-lung machine each time it is used in open-heart surgery.

Moreover, as many as 60 pints of blood may be needed for a single open-heart operation. In general, the acute need for blood has given rise to two types of blood banks:

A. *Commercial Blood Banks*

These are profit-making blood banks. In other words, they obtain blood supplies from donors who are paid. The blood is then processed and sold to hospitals at a profit.

B. *Community Blood Banks*

These are non-profit blood banks. Voluntary community donors supply them with their blood without stipulating a fee for this service. Sometimes these banks may demand that patients, upon recovery, replace 2 to 3 pints of blood transfused into them. It ought to be mentioned here that some hospitals possess their own blood banks.

C. *The Islamic Stance on Blood Banks*

Shaykh Abū Sinnah states that it is permissible (*jā'iz*) to collect blood from donors and preserve it in blood banks for the purpose of transfusing it into persons who are in acute need of it as a result of war, road and factory injuries. This permissibility is governed by the fact that blood banks do indeed safeguard the availability of blood in times of need.[30] He then derives support for his stance from the following which appears in *Kashshāf al-Qanā*ʿ:[31]

> Any person forced by necessity may store up what is (nutritionally) forbidden if he fears for his future needs in the event that he does not do so (i.e. store up). There is no harm in one's doing that nor in one's taking the necessary

> steps to prepare oneself to cope with and satisfy one's (essential) needs. However, it is not permissible for that person to partake of this until forced by necessity.[32]

Referring to blood which is stored in blood banks, the late Shaykh Jād al-Ḥaqq points out that it is permissible for one to pay a fee in order to receive blood transfusion from such institutions. The fee, however, should be viewed as compensation for its storage and collection and not as a sale. It is, therefore, imperative that this be mentioned in the documents of these institutions in order to allay any suspicion or doubt about the prohibition (of paying the stipulated fee).[33]

VII. The Religious Factor

Muftī Shafī' is of the view that it is preferable for a Muslim, as far as is feasible, to avoid having the blood of a non-Muslim transfused into him. He substantiates this by stating that the righteous persons of the *ummah* always discourage Muslim parents having their infants breastfed by women known to be of bad character. In other words, he feels that the blood recipient runs the risk of his character being affected negatively through the evil inclinations that permeate the blood of a rebellious sinner or unbeliever.[34]

Abū Sinnah does not touch on this issue. His colleague, 'Abd Allāh 'Abd al-Raḥmān al-Bassām, however, indirectly touches on this point when addressing the question of the permissibility of transplanting an organ belonging to a non-Muslim into the body of a Muslim. According to him there is no harm if that is done on account of the Muslim being in a state of dire need of that organ. He argues that the body of a Muslim as well as that of an unbeliever are both to be regarded as pure, when alive or dead. Thereafter, he substantiates this by stating that a Muslim man is permitted to marry a woman belonging to the People of the Book (i.e. a Jew or a Christian). Moreover, he explains the Qur'ānic verse *'Verily the* mushrikūn *(idolators) are nothing but unclean'* (al-Tawbah, 9:28) to mean that they are spiritually impure on account of their beliefs and associating partners with Allāh ﷻ. Then, in order to strengthen his case for such an interpretation, he quotes ʿAbd Allāh ibn ʿAbbās who made the following statement:

> *Shirk* (i.e. ascribing partners to Allah) is that which renders him (the *mushrik*) impure.[35]

It can therefore be said that Shaykh al-Bassām's legal verdict on the permissibility of a non-Muslim's organ being transplanted into a Muslim's body applies equally to the permissibility of the former's blood being transfused into the latter.

Part Three

Transplantation of Human Organs

CHAPTER 8

UTILISATION OF HUMAN PARTS IN ISLAMIC JURIDICAL LITERATURE

Transplantation of human organs, as is practised today, was certainly unknown to the classical Muslim jurists. However, the use of human parts for treatment or other purposes, was discussed by them. Their views on what, if any, uses may be made of parts of the human body and what benefit may legitimately be derived from such use, are clearly relevant to the contemporary issue of organ transplantation.

A. *The Ḥanafī School*

According to *Majmaʿ al-Anhār* it is detestable to use human or pig bones in treatment (procedures) in view of the fact that it is forbidden to derive any form of benefit from them.[1] Likewise, it is stated in the *Ḥāshiyah* of Ibn ʿĀbidīn that it is impermissible to sell anything that grows out from the human body, e.g. hair, nails, etc., since they constitute parts of the human being and hence it becomes incumbent upon one to bury them.[2]

B. *The Mālikī School*

According to *Bulghat al-Sālik* utilizing the nails of a dead person or any of the parts of his body (including the hair) is impermissible because these (parts) are regarded as sacred. Removing them would be a violation of the sanctity of the body.[3]

In *Qawānīn al-Aḥkām al-Sharīʿah* it is stated that it is impermissible to treat the body by utilizing anything that is regarded as forbidden in the same way as it is forbidden for one on the verge of starvation to consume human flesh.[4]

C. *The Shāfiʿī School*

According to *Mughnī al-Muḥtāj* it is forbidden for one to resort to cutting any part of the body so as to feed it to another person who is suffering from extreme hunger. This is so because doing so, even for the benefit of another (i.e. one whose life is in danger) would jeopardize one's own condition. In the same way, it would be impermissible for one whose life is in danger to excise a part of a living animal for his own benefit (i.e. in order to sustain his life).[5]

D. *The Ḥanbalī School*

The *Kashshāf al-Qināʿ* states that even for one whose life is in danger (i.e. through extreme hunger) it would be impermissible to kill another human being, be it a Muslim, *kāfir* or *dhimmī,*[6] or to excise a portion of that person so as to consume it, since the lives of both (the former and the latter) are equally honoured.[7]

E. *The Imāmiyyah School*

In the *Sharā'iʿ al-Islām* it is mentioned that it is forbidden for one whose life is in danger to excise a portion of a living human being for consumption because that would mean putting the life of the latter in danger.[8]

From the above, it is apparent that the factors relevant to the problem of utilizing parts of the human body pertain to its sacredness, and the belief that it is an *amānah* (trust) given to us by our Creator and should therefore not be subjected to any form of material end. These considerations have greatly influenced the thinking of certain Muslim scholars who oppose organ transplantation and their arguments are based on them, as will be discussed in the next chapter.

CHAPTER 9

VIEWS OF CONTEMPORARY MUSLIM SCHOLARS ON ORGAN TRANSPLANTATION

Insofar as organ transplantation itself is concerned one must bear in mind that both the Qur'ān and the *Sunnah* neither sanction it nor condemn it. Contemporary Muslim jurists have deliberated on the issue and proposed certain juristic guidelines based on deductions from the broad teachings of the two original sources of the *Sharīʿah*, namely, the Qur'ān and the *Sunnah*. As normally happens in all matters not specifically dealt with in these two original sources, there are differences of opinion among the jurists as will be illustrated in this chapter.

I. Opposing Viewpoints

Two prominent Muslim scholars who have written against organ transplantation are the late Muftī Muḥammad Shafīʿ of Pakistan and Dr ʿAbd al-Salām al-Shukrī of Egypt.

Muftī Shafīʿ holds organ transplantation as not permissible on the basis of the following principles: sacredness of human life/body; the human body being an *amānah* (trust); and finally that such a procedure would be tantamount to subjecting the human body to material ends.[1] These principles may be elucidated thus:

A. *Sacredness of Human Life/Body*

From the teachings of the Qur'ān it can be deduced that man is enjoined to protect and preserve his own life as well as that of others. For example, man is forbidden from taking his own life:

> *Do not kill or (destroy) yourselves: For verily Allah has been to you Most Merciful.* (al-Nisā', 4:29)
>
> *Make not your hands contribute to your own destruction.* (al-Baqarah, 2:195)

Likewise, the Qur'ān imbues in man the gravity of the sin for taking someone else's life:

> *If anyone slays a human being unless it be in legal punishment for murder or for spreading corruption on earth it shall be as if he had slain the whole of mankind; whereas if anyone saves a life, it shall be as if he had saved the life of all mankind.* (al-Mā'idah, 5:32)

In the *Ḥadīth* literature it is recorded that the Prophet Muḥammad ﷺ made the following declaration in his Farewell Sermon (*Khuṭbah al-Wadāʿ*):

> Your life and your property and your honour are sacred until you meet your Lord.[2]

The above-mentioned citations have led Muslim jurists to include any form of aggression that is directed, not only against the life of a human being but against parts of his/her body as a crime.[3] This view also gains support from the following *ḥadīth*:

> Breaking the bone of a dead person is equal in sinfulness and aggression to breaking it while a person is alive.[4]

In the light of the above *ḥadīth* the following questions may rightly be asked: How can one therefore be permitted to cut up a man's body and remove an organ from it? Would that not constitute an act of aggression against the human body and thus be tantamount to mutilation of the body?

B. *The Human Body as an* Amānah *(Trust)*

The Qur'ān (17:70; 21:20) tells us that Allah ﷻ has honoured man, made serviceable to him whatever is in the heavens and on earth as a blessing and mercy. Likewise, it also mentions that Allah ﷻ has endowed man with all that he is in need of in respect of bodily organs (90:8–9). This understanding would lead one to infer that man has no right to donate any of his organs since these organs are not in reality his own, but have rather been given to him as an *amānah* (trust).

C. *Subjecting the Human Body to Material Ends*

The impermissibility of subjecting the human body to material ends may be deduced from these two examples:

Firstly, from the *Fatāwā ʿĀlamgīriyyah*, it is stated that if a person, owing to hunger, finds himself on the verge of death, and is unable to find even the meat of a dead animal in order to save himself, and at that instant is offered human flesh, it would not be permissible for him to partake of it.[5]

Secondly, it is recorded in the *Ḥadīth* Literature that the Prophet Muḥammad ﷺ said that Allah ﷻ has denounced or cursed the one who joins the hair of a woman to that of another so as to make her hair appear long – and He ﷻ has also cursed the woman with whose hair such hair is joined.[6] While in the *Hidāyah*, it is stated that it is permissible for women to increase their locks by means of animal wool.[7] It may, therefore, be rightly inferred that the use of human hair for this purpose is unlawful. By extension, from the above two examples, the use of parts of the human body, i.e. organs, will also be unlawful.

Dr al-Shukrī makes a case against organ transplantation based on the following considerations:

i. SANCTITY OF THE HUMAN BODY

On the basis of this *ḥadīth*: 'Breaking the bone of a dead person is equal in sinfulness and aggression to breaking it while a person is alive', the *ʿulamā'* (Muslim scholars) make it a duty to re-inter human bones or remains if, for any reason, they are taken out of the graves. It is also equally obligatory to bury the limb that has been severed from a criminal, as well as human nails, hairs, etc. in honour of the sanctity of the human body.[8]

ii. PROHIBITION OF MAKING USE OF FORBIDDEN THINGS AS MEDICINES

The following *ḥadīth* of the Prophet ﷺ:

> Allah created the disease and also the cure and for every disease He has provided a cure. So treat yourselves with medicines, but do not treat yourselves with prohibited things.[9]

renders utilizing human organs in treatment procedures impermissible by virtue of the fact that, as already cited, the Ḥanafī school regards making use of human bones in treatment as detestable.[10]

iii. SAFEGUARDING THE HONOUR OF HUMAN LIFE

ʿAbd al-Raḥmān ibn ʿUthmān ؓ reports that a doctor came to the Prophet ﷺ and asked him about the permissibility of making use of frogs in medicines. The Prophet ﷺ forbade him from doing that.[11] Since this *ḥadīth* censures the killing of frogs so as to use them in medicines, would it not, therefore, be more deserving to safeguard the honour of human life by not allowing any human organs to be used in treatment procedures?[12]

iv. AVOIDING THE DOUBTFUL

In a *ḥadīth*, the Prophet ﷺ said:

> Both legal and illegal things are obvious, and in between them are doubtful matters. So whoever forsakes those doubtful things lest he may commit a sin will definitely avoid what is clearly illegal; and whoever indulges in these doubtful things boldly, is likely to commit what is clearly illegal. Sins are Allah's *ḥimā* (i.e. private pasture) and whoever pastures (his sheep) near it is likely to trespass in it at any moment.[13]

In the light of the above, utilizing human organs in transplantation procedures would be tantamount to indulging in the doubtful. Thus if one were to avoid resorting to organ transplantation one would benefit in two ways. Firstly, if organ transplantation were to fall within the prohibited category, then one would have safeguarded oneself from exceeding the limits set by Allah ﷻ. Secondly, if organ transplantation were to be within the permissible category then one would be rewarded for having avoided it lest it might be within the perimeters of the forbidden.[14]

II. Favourable Viewpoints

To date, no Muslim scholar has offered to write an argument unreservedly in favour of organ transplantation. However, Muslim scholars in various parts of the world have either written arguments in favour or issued positive religious decrees (*fatāwā*) on the issue.

Muslim scholars who advocate the permissibility of organ transplantation are of the opinion that it should be recognized as a form of altruistic service to fellow Muslims.[15] Their stance on organ transplantation may be summarized as follows:

A. Al-Maṣlaḥah *(Public Welfare)*

It is true that Islam forbids any act of aggression against human life as well as the body after death. Thus if one were to take an organ out of the dead man's body so as to transplant it into another person, it could justifiably be argued to be tantamount to mutilation of the body and violation of the sanctity of the corpse. However, it is to be noted here that the Islamic legal system takes the interests of man into consideration. This accounts for the following juridical rules:[16]

i. Necessity makes the unlawful permissible.
ii. When two interests conflict let the one which will bring greater benefit take precedence.
iii. If forced to choose, choose the lesser of the two evils.

The above rules are founded on the principles of establishing what is in the general interest and preventing what is against it. So, if the general gain outweighs the negative aspect of an action, it is allowed, but if the negative consequences of such an action outweigh the good, then it is prohibited.

In this context, for example, Islamic Law would permit the cutting of the belly of the dead pregnant woman in order to remove the foetus should any movement be detected.[17] Thus, the right of the living supersedes consideration over the dead.

Likewise, Islamic Law would allow the cutting of the belly of the deceased who had swallowed a valuable diamond or a piece of gold in order that it may be returned to its rightful owner. The logical explanation for this is that if the valuable article had belonged to the deceased himself then his heirs would be in a position to benefit from it.[18]

Hence, following the same line of argument, after a person has died, it would be justified to retrieve the desired organ from that person's body for the purpose of transplanting it into that of another living person. This act would be regarded as a commendable gesture since as a result of this procedure, the quality of life of the living would be enhanced.

It ought to be noted, however, that Muslim scholars who advocate the permissibility of organ transplantation do not give outright approval for the practice. They are of the view that the permissibility of organ transplantation should be hedged with certain restrictions as enumerated below:[19]

1. That the transplantation is the only form (means) of treatment.
2. The expected degree of success of this procedure is relatively high.
3. The consent of the owner of the organ or of his heirs has been obtained.
4. Death must have been fully established by Muslim doctors of upright character before such a venture is undertaken.
5. The recipient has been informed of the operation and its implication.

B. Al-Īthār *(Altruism)*

The Qur'ān and the *Sunnah* exhort Muslims to co-operate with one another and to strengthen the bond of brotherhood among them. The Qur'ānic imperative in this regard is:

> *Help you one another in righteousness and piety.* (al-Mā'idah, 5:2)

and from the *Sunnah* the following *ḥadīth* may be cited:

> The believers, in their love and sympathy for one another, are like a whole body; when one part of it is affected with pain the whole of it responds in terms of wakefulness and fever.[20]

Thus in the light of the above teachings, a living person's gesture to donate one of his organs to a sibling or another person who may be in dire need of it should be viewed as an act of altruism, of some people sharing what they have for the benefit of others. Here again, the following restrictions should be taken heed of:[21]

1. The consent of the donor must be obtained.
2. That the transplantation is the only form of treatment possible.
3. That there is no imminent danger to the life of the donor.
4. The respective transplantation has been proven successful in the past.

Moreover, it should be noted that a vital organ (like the heart) cannot be donated in view of the fact that this would result in the death of the donor. The late Shaykh Jād al-Ḥaqq explains that this prohibition has no exception, whether the one from whom the vital organ is taken has given his/her permission or not. If that person gave permission for the transplantation of his/her vital organ into someone else's body this would be tantamount to suicide. On the other hand, if that person had not given any consent for his/her vital organ to be transplanted into someone else's body then the people who undertake doing that would be guilty of taking the life of that person without any justifiable cause.[22] To protect one's life and organs is an obligation. Thus one cannot prefer the life of another over one's own except if it be for a higher objective like the protection of the *dīn* (Islamic Faith) by giving one's life in *jihād* (for the defence of Islam).[23]

C. *Sale of Organs*

Insofar as the selling of human organs is concerned, Muslim scholars concur that such sale would be deemed *bāṭil* (i.e. null and void)[24] based on the following considerations:

i. A person cannot trade in something of which he is not the owner.[25]
ii. A *ḥadīth* which states that: 'Amongst those who would be held accountable on the Last Day is one who sold a freeman and ate up the proceeds.'[26]

   Thus if one were to sell a freeman, the buyer would have no right over him during his lifetime since the contract of sale was *ḥarām* (prohibited) from the very outset. The body of a person, living or dead, belongs to Allah ﷻ alone. It follows, therefore, that no one, and not even one's progeny, has any right to sell, donate or dispose of another person's body (organs included) except in the manner prescribed by Islam, that is, by proper burying of the deceased.
iii. Such a practice would lead to abuse in the sense that it could result in the organs of the poor being sold in the market like any other commodity.[27]

D. *Non-Muslim Organs*

The permissibility for Muslims to receive the organs of non-Muslims is based on the following two conditions:[28]

1. No organs are available from Muslims.
2. A Muslim's life would be in danger should the transplantation not be carried out.

In order to circumvent the problem of Muslims becoming recipients of non-Muslim organs, some contemporary Muslim jurists are of the opinion that a Muslim's gesture in donating any of his organs is to be categorized as *farḍ kifāyah*[29] (a collective obligation if fulfilled by the few absolves the generality).

CHAPTER 10

ISLAMIC JURIDICAL RESOLUTIONS ON ORGAN TRANSPLANTATION

As far as religious decrees (*fatāwā*) on contemporary problems are concerned, there exist in Saudi Arabia and India independent juridical academies under the name *al-Majmaʿ al-Fiqhī al-Islāmī* (Islamic Juridical Academy) which meet at regular intervals in order to deliberate on a variety of issues affecting Muslims in their social, political and economic spheres of life. In this chapter only the resolutions on organ transplantation issued by these bodies will be discussed.

I. Saudi Arabian Juridical Academies

In Saudi Arabia, there are two Islamic Fiqh Academies. One of them is based in Makkah and the other in Jeddah. The Makkan academy functions under the auspices of *Rābiṭah al-ʿĀlam al-Islāmī* (Muslim World League) and certain prominent Muslim scholars from all over the world have been co-opted as its members. Its religious decrees are issued in its journal *Majallat al-Majmaʿ al-Fiqhī* which is published bi-annually. The Jeddah academy is an organ of the Organization of Islamic Conference (OIC). Its officials are drawn from member-states and from some other countries.[1] Its resolutions and recommendations are collated and published.

II. Islamic Fiqh Academy of India

Al-Majmaʿ al-Fiqhī al-Islāmī (Islamic Juridical Academy) of India, was founded by the renowned Muslim religious scholar,

Qāḍī Mujāhid al-Islām. It is based in the state of Bihar in India. This academy holds at least two seminars on Islamic juridical issues every year in different cities throughout India.[2] Its proceedings are published in its quarterly Urdu journal, *Baḥth-o-Naẓar* (Research and Studies).[3]

A. *Resolutions on Autotransplant*

The Council of the Islamic Fiqh Academy of the Muslim World League, Makkah, at its eighth working session (1405 AH/1985) resolved that it is permissible within the *Sharīʿah* to take a part of the human body and transplant it into the same body like removing the skin or bone in order to graft it to some other part of that same body.[4]

The Council of the Islamic Fiqh Academy of the Organization of Islamic Conference, Jeddah, Saudi Arabia, at its fourth working session (1408 AH/1988) resolved that from the *Sharīʿah* point of view an organ may be transplanted from one part of the body to another part of that same body, provided it could be ascertained that the benefits accruing from this procedure would outweigh the harmful effects of it. Furthermore, it resolved that it is also permissible for such a procedure to be undertaken for the purpose of replacing a lost organ, or reshaping it, or restoring its function, or correcting a defect, or removing a malformation which was the source of mental anguish or physical pain.[5]

The Islamic Fiqh Academy of India, at its first Islamic Jurisprudence Seminar (Delhi, March 1989), resolved that it is valid to replace a part of a person's body with another part from the same person on the ground of necessity.[6]

B. *Resolutions on Homotransplant/Allotransplant*

The Council of the Islamic Fiqh Academy of the Muslim World League, Makkah, at its eighth working session (1405 AH/1985) resolved that it is permissible within the *Sharīʿah* to remove the organ from one person and transplant it into another person's body in order to save the life of that person or to assist in stabilizing the normal functioning of the basic organs of that person. Likewise, the Academy pointed out that such a procedure does in no way violate the dignity of the person from whose body the organ had been removed. Hence, the act of donating one's organ is to be viewed as a permissible and praiseworthy act as long as the following conditions are met:

i. That the donor's life is not harmed in any way;
ii. That the donor voluntarily donates his/her organ without any form of coercion;
iii. That the procedure is the only medical means available to alleviate the plight of the patient;
iv. That the success rate of the procedures for removing and transplanting the organ is relatively high.[7]

The Islamic Fiqh Academy of India, at its first *Fiqh* (Islamic Jurisprudence) Seminar (Delhi, March 1989), resolved that transplantation of a human organ is permissible in a desperate and unavoidable situation wherein the patient's organ has stopped functioning and there is present danger that he/she would lose his/her life if the organ were not replaced. Likewise, it is also permissible for a healthy person, in the light of the opinion of medical experts, to donate one of his/her kidneys to an ailing relative.[8] Insofar as corneal transplant is concerned, the Council of the Islamic Fiqh Academy of the Organization of Islamic Conference, Jeddah, Saudi Arabia, at its fourth working session (1408 AH/1988) resolved that from the *Sharīʿah* point of view such a procedure is permissible.[9]

C. *Resolution on Heterotransplant*

The Council of the Islamic Fiqh Academy of the Muslim World League, Makkah, Saudi Arabia, at its eighth working session (1405 AH/1985) resolved that it is permissible within the *Sharīʿah* to transplant the organ of an animal which has been slaughtered according to Islamic rites and/or that of other animals out of necessity.[10] This resolution on heterotransplants was also ratified by the Islamic Fiqh Academy of India, at its first Islamic Jurisprudence Seminar (Delhi, March 1989).[11]

From the above resolutions, it appears that there is consensus among the different Islamic juridical bodies that a Muslim, while living, may donate one of his organs, but not a vital one such as the heart. Equally, a Muslim may become the recipient of human or animal organs. This brings us to the question as to whether it would be permissible for a Muslim to make a will, while still alive, stipulating his/her consent to donate his/her organ after death; or alternatively who would have the jurisdiction to assent to the donation of the dead person's organ in the event that no such clause has been stipulated in the deceased's will.

CHAPTER 11

THE INCLUSION OF ORGAN DONATION IN ONE'S WILL

Al-Waṣiyyah is the Arabic equivalent of what today is termed as the last will and testament. The drafting of such a will during one's lifetime is Divinely ordained. The Qur'ānic imperative in this regard is as follows:

> *O you who believe! When death approaches any of you, (take) witnesses among yourselves when making bequests, two just men of your own (kindred) or others from outside (your kindred) if you are journeying...* (al-Mā'idah, 5:106)

Likewise, the Prophet Muḥammad ﷺ also emphasized the need to write down one's will. He said:

> It is not right for any Muslim person, who has anything to bequeath, that he may pass even two nights without having his last will and testament written and kept ready with him.[1]

However, it ought to be noted here that according to Islamic Law, the proportionate shares that the legal heirs receive from the deceased's estate are neither dependent on a will nor on any other direction of the deceased. Rather, these shares are governed by certain rules that have been laid down in the Islamic law of inheritance.[2] Thus what can be included in a will are certain specific stipulations, for example that which relate to the affairs of the testator's young children, facilitating the marriage of the testator's daughters, and the devolution of one-third of the testator's estate[3] in favour of a particular person or a charitable institution.

Today, as already discussed in the previous chapters, modern science has made it possible to harvest the organ of the deceased and to transplant it into the living for the purpose of improving the latter's quality of life. The question that arises here is whether it is permissible for the testator to include organ donation in his/her will?

As no explicit *naṣṣ* (text) exists either in the Qur'ān or in the *Sunnah* on this question, differences of opinion prevail among Muslim scholars.

I. Negative Resolution

The Islamic Fiqh Academy of India, during its Second *Fiqh* Seminar, held 8–11 December 1989 at the Hamdard Convention Centre, New Delhi, resolved that if a person directed that after his death his organ should be used for the purpose of transplantation (testamentary disposition, as is commonly known), it would not be considered as *waṣiyyah* (will) according to *Sharīʿah*.[4]

The arguments that may have influenced the adoption of this negative resolution are based on, firstly, the concept that human organs are an *amānah* from the Creator and, secondly, to the stance that human organs cannot be valued or priced in the way that human possessions can.

A. *Human Organ: An* Amānah

As discussed in Chapter 9, there are Muslim jurists who regard the human body (including its parts) as an *amānah* (trust). Therefore, since a human being does not own his body, he/she cannot make a gift in respect of any part of his/her body either during his/her lifetime or after death. Thus to include organ donation in one's will would not be in order since one cannot give away that which one does not legally own.

B. *Human Organ: Invaluable*

The testator's estate is termed in Arabic *māl mutaqawwam* (asset upon which a price can be set). Muslim jurists are of the opinion that a human being's person (organs included) is *māl ghayr mutaqawwam* (not able to be valued, i.e. no price can be set for it).[5] Thus it logically follows that since no price can be set for a human organ, the stipulation for it to be donated after one's death, is null and void.

II. Positive Resolutions

The Council of the Islamic Fiqh Academy of the Muslim World League, Makkah, at its eighth working session (1405 AH/1985), resolved that it is permissible in *Sharīʿah* to remove an organ from a dead person and transplant it into a living recipient, on the condition that the donor was sane (*mukallaf*) and had wished it so.[6]

The Council of the Islamic Fiqh Academy of the Organization of Islamic Conference (OIC), during its fourth session held in Jeddah, (1988) resolved that it is permissible from the *Sharīʿah* point of view to transplant an organ from the body of a dead person if it is essential to keep the beneficiary alive, or if it restores a basic function to his body, provided it has been authorized by the deceased or by his heirs after his death or with the permission of concerned authorities if the deceased has not been identified or has no heirs.[7]

The above (positive) resolutions, we may safely assume, provide a valid theoretical basis for the inclusion of organ donation in one's will. The considerations that have played a major role in influencing the adoption of these positive resolutions for the inclusion of organ donation in one's will relate to what are termed as (a) *al-Īthār* (altruism, i.e. generosity towards humankind) and (b) *al-ḍarūrah* (the rule of necessity).

A. Al-Īthār *(Altruism)*

This consideration was discussed in Chapter 9. Here we may add that a living person's gesture in willing to donate his/her cornea, for example, after death has taken place should be viewed as an act of altruism. After all, through corneal transplant the donor would in effect have made a noble contribution in restoring the sight of another fellow human being suffering from corneal blindness.

B. Al-Ḍarūrah *(The Rule of Necessity)*

Dr Tanzīlur Raḥmān, former Chief Justice of Pakistan, is of the opinion that the inclusion of corneal donation, for example, in one's will may be held permissible on the basis of the rule of necessity. He explains that the rule of necessity is based upon the juridical principle of *al-Istiḥsān* (juristic preference), that the needs of the living are given preference over those of the dead.[8] Thus the inclusion of organ donation in one's will could be a positive step in resolving organ donation shortages worldwide.

III. The Enforceable Nature of Such a Will

The Islamic Fiqh Academy of India, as pointed out above, resolved that any direction cited in the will pertaining to the donation of one's organ for transplantation would be invalid and should not be honoured.[9]

Dr Tanzīlur Raḥmān holds the view that once a person has included organ donation in his/her will, it will be valid and enforceable in *Sharīʿah*, subject to the following conditions:[10]

i. The donation (by will) is motivated purely for human good and is without any monetary or other renumeration.
ii. The recipient's need is genuine, of the nature of extreme and dire necessity, with no alternative treatment available, and duly certified by two Muslim medical practitioners of integrity.
iii. The legator (donor) leaves behind no heir. In case there is an heir, obtaining his consent, after death, shall be necessary. If any one of the heirs, there being more than one heir, does not consent to it, the will shall not be executed.

iv. In case the will is in respect of eyes, the eyes are to be taken out or separated from the body, after certification of death by two Muslim medical practitioners of integrity, to the extent of need as per the will, only before burial of the dead body and no insult nor unecessary disfiguring should be done to the dead body.[11]

Insofar as who would have the authority to assent to a donation of a dead person's organs in the event that no such clause has been stipulated in the deceased's will, the Council of the Islamic Fiqh Academy of the Organization of Islamic Conference and Dr Tanzīlur Raḥmān concur that the legal heirs could give the necessary assent for that.

CHAPTER 12

HUMAN CLONING

Cloning is the technique of producing a genetically identical duplicate of an organism. A clone is thus the asexual progeny of a single individual. After the successful cloning of Dolly the sheep in 1997, scientists are of the opinion that in the not so distant future human cloning will become a reality. Human cloning will require taking a somatic cell, not a reproductive cell (like egg or sperm cell), from a person and the DNA from the cell is removed and transferred to an unfertilized egg taken from a second woman, whose nucleus, its DNA, had been removed, eliminating all genetic characteristics of the egg donor. An electrical charge is applied to the egg which tricks it into believing that it has been fertilized and so it will start to divide.[1] The fertilized egg is then implanted into a surrogate mother. The resulting baby will be genetically identical to the original somatic cell donor.

I. Therapeutic Uses of Cloning Technology

Cloning technology is expected to benefit mankind, especially in the field of medicine. Some of the therapeutic benefits of cloning technology may be summarized as follows:

- Human cloning could make it possible for many more infertile couples to have children.
- Human organs could be cloned selectively for use as replacement organs for host individuals, thus eliminating the risk of rejection.
- Cells could be cloned and regenerated to replace damaged tissues of the body, e.g. nerve or muscle tissues.

- Using cloning technology, medical scientists may be in a position to switch cells on and off through cloning and thus it may be possible to cure cancer.
- Through cloning technology it may in time be possible to test for and cure genetic diseases.

II. Muslim Concerns

The concerns which Muslims have in regard to human cloning may be summarized as follows: Firstly, does human cloning affect one's belief in Allah ﷻ as the Creator? Secondly, will such an innovation undermine family relationships and responsibilities? Finally, is it justified to benefit from therapeutic uses of human cloning?

A. *Belief in Allah ﷻ as the Creator*

There are many passages in the Qur'ān which deal with the various stages of human creation. In one such passage it is stated:

> *We created you out of dust, and then out of a drop of semen, and then out of a germ-cell, and then out of an embryonic lump, completely formed, and yet incomplete, so that We make your origin clear unto you. Whatever We will, We cause to rest in the (mothers') wombs for a term set by Us.* (al-Ḥajj, 22:5)

From this passage it seems that the Qur'ānic paradigm of creation pre-empts any move towards cloning. From the beginning of life to the point of death it is a Divine act. Any replication would then simply be considered a redundant exercise. It was obvious then that when Dolly the sheep came into existence asexually, the very first question that was raised was: Does this scientific accomplishment affect our belief in Allah ﷻ as the Creator? The answer is of course in the negative in view of the fact that the Qur'ān tells us that Allah ﷻ created the Prophet Adam عليه السلام without a father and mother and the Prophet Jesus عليه السلام without a father:

> *The similitude of Jesus before Allah is that of Adam; He created him from dust, then said to him: 'Be', and he was.* (Āl ʿImrān, 3:59)
>
> *... the angel said: 'O Mary! Allah gives you glad tidings of a word from Him: his name will be the Messiah Jesus, son of Mary, held in honour in this world and the Hereafter and of (the company of) those nearest to Allah.*
>
> *He shall speak to the people from in the cradle and in maturity, and he is of the company of the righteous.'*
>
> *She said: 'O my Lord! How shall I have a son when no man has touched me?' He (the angel) said: 'Thus it is: Allah creates what He wills. When He wills a thing to be, He but says unto it 'Be', and it is.'* (Āl ʿImrān, 3:45–7)

What is evident from the above Qur'ānic citations is that everything happens according to the Divine Will. However, while Allah ﷻ has established a system of cause and effect in this Universe, one cannot rule out that He has also made provisions for exceptions to this general rule as in the case of the creation of Prophets Adam ﷺ and Jesus ﷺ. If human cloning is ever to become a reality, it will be so in accordance to the Divine Will. Moreover, if this biotechnological manipulation proves successful, it will not in any way compromise our belief in Allah ﷻ as the Ultimate Creator in view of the fact that the primary materials, namely the somatic cell and the unfertilized egg, are both the result of the handiwork of Allah ﷻ. Furthermore, it is interesting to note that some Muslim scientists are of the view that this new biotechnological accomplishment may well assist in strengthening our faith (*īmān*) in the Resurrection when Allah ﷻ will raise us from the dead to stand in judgement before Him ﷻ in the life to come.[2]

B. *Family Relationship*

Islam recognizes spousal relationship through marriage as the cornerstone for the creation of a Divinely-ordained society.

Children born in wedlock carry the genetic components of both parents and it is this genetic combination that gives them their identity. Consequently, the concern that Muslims have is that this form of genetic replication will negatively impact upon spousal and child-parent relationship and bring an end to the Islamic family institution. Moreover, human cloning will rob the child of his/her roots (ancestry) and undermine the Islamic laws of inheritance which are based on consanguinity.[3]

C. *Benefitting from Therapeutic Uses of Human Cloning*

In order to be in a position to determine whether it would be justified, under the *Sharīʿah*, to derive benefit from the therapeutic uses of human cloning, one would have to evaluate the benefits *vis-à-vis* the harm. With that end in mind, some of the therapeutic uses of human cloning are hereunder described:

i. CURING DISEASES

Cloning technology could in future assist in finding cures for cancer, reverse heart attacks, and manufacture bone, fat, connective tissue or cartilage that matches the patient's tissues for the purpose of reconstructive and cosmetic surgery. It would, in the opinion of the author, be permissible to undertake research in human cloning in order to find cures or to unlock the mysteries of the diseases which are today regarded as incurable. The *ḥadīth*: 'For every disease there is a cure'[4] could provide justification for undertaking such research. However, it should be stressed that it would contravene the sanctity of life to test the cloned embryos for genetic diseases for the purpose of destroying all those which test positive.[5]

ii. INFERTILITY

While it is true that human cloning will resolve the problem of infertility, one has to take cognisance of the fact that Ian Wilmut, A.E. Schnieke, J. McWhir, A.J. Kind and K.H.S. Campbell made

277 attempts before they finally succeeded in cloning Dolly. Human cloning will inevitably be a more complex procedure. During the initial experimentation to produce a viable clone, it will result in many more miscarriages and deaths. Moreover, out of the many embryos that would be created only one would finally be implanted into a surrogate mother and all others would be discarded or destroyed. This would then pose a serious problem in that destruction of the embryos is a crime according to the *Sharīʿah*.[6] Furthermore, cloning technology tampers with the *Sunan* of Allah (Divine Pattern) in the normal process of procreation of humans, i.e. to reproduce without a sexual partner and this undermines the institution of marriage.[7] Production of human clones will also, as pointed out above, negatively impact upon the Islamic laws of inheritance (*al-mīrāth*).

iii. ORGANS FOR TRANSPLANTATION

The possibility exists that, in time, people may have their diseased tissues replaced with cloned embryo tissues or damaged organs replaced with those of other human clones. This manipulation to derive benefit from human clones will be considered a crime under Islamic Law because it contravenes the sanctity of life.[8] However, if it is at all possible to regrow body parts, then there would be no objection from the *Sharīʿah* to make use of this procedure in order to regrow the limbs of those who lost any of their limbs as a result, for example, of falling victims to land mines or other forms of accident. But it would become questionable to regrow the limbs of those whose limbs have been amputated in accordance with the dictates of the *Sharīʿah* for certain crimes.[9]

iv. REVERSING THE AGING PROCESS

It is believed that some day it will be possible to reverse the aging process because of what we learn from cloning. This contradicts the *ḥadīth* in which the following incident is reported:

> The Bedouin Arabs came to the Prophet ﷺ and said, 'O Messenger of Allah should we treat ourselves?' He replied, 'Yes, O servants of Allah, you must treat (yourselves) for verily, Allah did not create a disease without providing a cure for it, except one disease.' They asked him, 'Which one?' He replied, 'Old age.'[10]

v. SALE OF EMBRYOS AND BODY CELLS

A market could develop for the sale of cloned embryos and body cells. Any such transaction would be deemed *bāṭil* (i.e. null and void) based on the following considerations:

i. A person cannot trade in something of which he is not the owner.[11]
ii. A *ḥadīth* which states that: 'Amongst those who would be held accountable on the Last Day is one who sold a freeman and ate up the proceeds.'[12]

Thus the potential harm of human cloning technology far outweighs any good that may accrue from it and thus it would not be justified for Muslims to benefit from therapeutic uses of human cloning.

III. Resolutions of the Islamic Fiqh Academy on Human Cloning

The Islamic Fiqh Academy of the Muslim World League at its tenth meeting held in Jeddah, (1418 AH/1997) unanimously resolved that:[13]

1. The cloning of humans is un-Islamic and should be strictly forbidden, no matter what methods are used to produce identical humans.
2. If the *Sharīʿah* restriction pertaining to No. 1 above is transgressed, the consequences of human cloning will have to be reviewed in the light of the *Sharīʿah*.

3. All (biotechnological) manipulations (involving human procreation) whereby a third party element is introduced (outside the marital bounds), be that in the form of womb, egg, sperm or cell, are unlawful.
4. It is permissible to make use of cloning technology and genetic engineering in the domain of germ, micro-organism, plant or animal life, within the parameters of the *Sharīʿah*, for the purpose of promoting that which would be of general benefit and would in no way result in causing any harm.
5. An open call is made to all Islamic States to legislate laws and necessary regulations in order to close the doors, directly or indirectly, to prevent local and foreign agencies, foreign organizations and foreign experts from using the Islamic countries as bases to carry out experimentation in the field of human cloning for the sake of their own propaganda.
6. There should be close co-operation between the Islamic Fiqh Academy and the Islamic Medical Organization on the issue of cloning. Members of these two organizations should acquaint and familiarize themselves with the latest scientific discussions and technical terminologies. They should also hold conferences and regular seminars in order to elucidate the *Sharīʿah* position on the issue of cloning.
7. Invitation should be extended to form specialized committees comprising scientific experts and *Sharīʿah* scholars in order to formulate ethical guidelines for conducting research and experimentations in the biological sciences with the aim of implementing such guidelines in the Islamic States.
8. It called for the establishment and financing of specialized research institutions which would be entrusted to carry out research in the biological sciences and genetic engineering, within the parameters of the

Sharīʿah, excluding research in the field of human cloning. This will enable the Islamic world to conduct independent research and end their dependence upon the scientific findings of others.

9. The mass media are called upon to project the Islamic view alongside the new scientific findings. Every effort should be made by the mass media not to disseminate any misinformation about Islam. In compliance with the directive of Allah ﷻ, all reports should be scrutinized before they are disseminated:

   > *And when there comes to them some matter touching (public) safety or fear, they divulge it. If they had only referred it to the Messenger or to those charged with authority among them, the proper investigators would have known it from them (direct). Were it not for the Grace and Mercy of Allah unto you, all but a few of you would have followed Satan.* (al-Nisāʼ, 4:83)

Part Four

The Moment of Death

CHAPTER 13

MEDICAL SCIENCE AND THE DETERMINATION OF DEATH

Death is an inevitable reality but the causes leading to death may vary from individual to individual. The human body is a group of cells, organs and systems. A disorder in the function of an organ affects the systematic functioning of other organs as well. Since organs and cells require oxygen for nourishment, they are dependent upon the respiratory system to provide them with the necessary oxygen. Failure to receive their supply of oxygen due to the malfunctioning of the respiratory system or failure of the heart to pump blood to the organs will lead to deterioration of the organs and result in the eventual death of the individual. Likewise, if medical intervention is not undertaken to rectify kidney failure it will frustrate the body's ability to dispose of its waste and in due course the person will die. A person who commits suicide by hanging experiences immediate death in view of the fact that once the brain stem is deprived of an oxygenated blood supply it becomes irreversibly damaged due to the ripping off of the upper cervical vertebrae where the brain stem is located. Cardiac arrest follows brain stem death, although pulse rate will still be able to be felt for a few minutes thereafter.[1]

In the past, death was considered to be a simple and straightforward phenomenon. The general practitioner would issue the death certificate once he was convinced that there was cessation or absence of spontaneous life in the patient. This meant that the patient had stopped breathing, his heart had stopped beating, there was unresponsiveness, his body had turned cold and finally rigor mortis had set in.[2]

With the successful accomplishment of heart transplantation, it became obvious that determining the moment of death now required further thought. Cessation of heart beat is no longer considered evidence of death since the heart can now be substituted with that of a just-deceased donor or with that of a baboon or even with a mechanical one. Moreover, modern biomedical innovations like the resuscitator and cardiac pacemaker have made it imperative to establish a set of criteria by which the moment of death can be identified.[3]

I. The Process of Dying

Frank J. Ayd describes death as 'an orderly progression from clinical death to brain death, to biological death, to cellular death.'[4] This may be elucidated as follows:

- Clinical death occurs when the body's vital functions – respiration and heartbeat – wane and finally cease.[5] Clinical death may in some cases be reversed. For example, a child who has drowned and is pulled out of water without heartbeat and respiration can be saved through the initiation of mouth-to-mouth resuscitation and cardiac massage.[6]
- Brain death occurs after cardiac and respiratory arrest because under normal temperature conditions, the human brain cannot survive loss of oxygen for more than ten minutes.[7] Ayd points out that as a result of anoxia (oxygen starvation), the component parts of the brain die in progressive steps. Death of the cortex is followed by that of the midbrain (diencephalon) and finally ending with the brain stem. When the whole brain has died, biological death takes place. Biological death is denoted by the absence of bodily movements. A dead brain cannot sustain bodily life. Once bodily life ceases, cellular death follows.[8]

From the above, it is clear that death occurs progressively and that the death of the brain is the determining factor in the process of dying. Dr Aḥmad al-Qāḍī of Akbar Clinic, Panama City, Florida, USA, aptly explains that:

Any other organ may die or be surgically removed and yet the owner continues to live, retaining his reason, power of thinking, awareness, personality, and everything else, either because the organ concerned is one that a person can live without such as the limbs, parts of the stomach or the intestines, and so on or because of the availability of a replacement which can carry on the functions of that organ for a long or short period of time.[9]

The brain is a different kind of organ altogether. The brain cells, as Harmon L. Smith points out, are extremely sensitive to anoxia. Thus the cerebral cortical cells begin to die within five minutes, if deprived of oxygenated blood, and death of the whole brain results thereafter within approximately the next ten minutes. The other vital organs like the heart, for example, can be reactivated after several minutes of cessation; the kidneys can still be viable after the lapse of one hour following nephrectomy; and corneal transplants can still be carried out although several days may have elapsed since they had been surgically removed.[10] Moreover, unlike the other vital organs, the brain cannot be replaced in view of the fact that a sound living brain can only be found in a living person and it will not be possible to find a substitute to the human brain in the foreseeable or distant future. It is for this reason that modern medical science holds that brain death determines the end of human life. This is confirmed in a statement made by M. Goulon and P. Babinet:

> The brain only gives man his reality; where it has disappeared, man no longer is. Such is also the opinion expressed by the leading national and international medical authorities.[11]

Furthermore, the observation made by Dr Mukhtār al-Mahdī, a neurosurgeon, may be relevant to the understanding of brain death:

> Damaged brain cells are irreplaceable. But by resorting to the ventilator, the organs of the body other than the brain may be kept alive for a period of time ranging from a few

hours to two weeks, more or less. But that period cannot go on much longer even if we continue to give the patient all the stimulating aids possible. Blood pressure would begin to drop, food assimilation process would slow down, body temperature would drop, and finally the heart would stop.[12]

II. Diagnosis of Brain Death

It is important to point out here that a vegetative state should not be confused with the diagnosis of brain death. Vegetative patients are able to breathe spontaneously; at times, they can follow objects with their eyes; they do respond to painful stimuli and in due course may even recover from their neurological disability. Thus patients suffering from irreversible coma are certified brain dead only after stringent tests have been carried out on them. These tests will confirm the patients' unresponsiveness to painful stimuli; their pupils' non-reaction to light, their remaining fixed and dilated; their inability to swallow, yawn or vocalize; and their inability to breathe spontaneously within a three-minute period after the ventilator is switched off. Flat electro encephalogram (EEG) will further verify the absence of electric waves being transmitted by the brain. Extreme caution is taken before finally pronouncing them brain dead in that these clinical examinations are repeated at intervals to ensure that there is no improvement in the patients' condition.[13] In the event that organ donation is envisaged, upon confirmation of brain death diagnosis, the patients are reconnected to the ventilator, and kept in the intensive therapy unit (ITU) until the transplant surgery can be carried out.[14] Vital organs, for example, heart, lungs, kidneys and liver, of brain dead patients have a better chance of functioning in the post-operative period. This, however, should not lead us to believe that the motivation behind declaring patients brain dead is conditioned by the interest of transplant surgeons to harvest the organs for transplantation purposes. As a matter of fact, the physicians who are to be associated with the subsequent organ transplantation are precluded from the diagnosis of brain death.[15]

CHAPTER 14

THE QUR'ĀNIC CONCEPT OF DEATH

The Qur'ān, emphasizing the universality of death, uses the expression *'every soul is bound to taste death,'* (Āl ʿImrān, 3:185) thus signifying that all that exists will die *'but will abide (forever) the Face of your Lord, full of Majesty, Bounty and Honour'* (al-Raḥmān, 55:27).

In several passages, the Qur'ān affirms that both life and death are in the control of Allah ﷾. For example, it states:

> *Say (O Muḥammad): Allah gives you life, then causes you to die...* (al-Jāthiyah, 45:26)

According to Ibn Kathīr, the renowned *mufassir* (exegetist) of the Qur'ān, this verse was revealed in order to impress upon the Quraysh, who denied the existence of life after death and attributed all earthly events to Time (*al-dahr*), that Allah ﷾ is the One Who exercises control over everything.[1]

The Qur'ān makes mention of the *rūḥ* (the spirit) being breathed into every human being during the process of being created as cited in the following verse:

> *He made all things good which He creates, and He began the creation of man from clay. Then He made his seed* (naslahū) *from a quantity* (sulālatin) *of lowly fluids. Then He fashioned him and breathed into him from His Spirit* (rūḥihī)... (al-Sajdah, 32:7–9)

The Qur'ān also informs us that death as an event occurs when the *nafs* (the soul) is separated from the body as in the following citation:

> *Allah takes the souls* (anfus) *at the time of death.* (al-Zumar, 39:42)

The Arabic operative verb *yatawaffā* has been used in the above mentioned Qur'ānic verse in order to designate death and this term implies both 'seizing' or 'causing to die'.[2]

It may be noted here that the two Qur'ānic terms, namely *rūḥ* (pl. *arwāḥ*) and *nafs* (pl. *anfus),* are synonymous (even if they are translated as spirit and soul respectively) and imply one and the same thing, i.e. the soul. This is pointed out by Muḥammad al-Ḥusayn al-Dāmaghānī in his *Qāmūs al-Qur'ān* (Dictionary of the Qur'ān).[3] Hence, in the *Ḥadīth* literature we come across an incident whereby the Prophet Muḥammad ﷺ came to Abū Salamah as he died. He noticed that his eyes were fixedly open, so he closed them and said: 'When the soul (*rūḥ*) is taken away (i.e. at the time of death) the sight follows it…'[4]

Death as a process is signified by the Qur'ānic term *ajal* as is evident in the following citation:

> *But to no soul will Allah grant respite when its appointed time* (ajaluhā) *has come; and Allah is well acquainted with all that you do.* (al-Munāfiqūn, 63:11)

The Arabic-English Lexicon explains that the term *ajal* implies 'the duration of life: and its end: a man's life being thus termed: and his death by which it terminates: the assigned or appointed duration of the life of man.'[5]

Thus, according to the Qur'ān, death is something that is pre-determined and fixed by Allah ﷻ as categorically stated in the following verse:

> *And no human being can die save by Allah's leave, at a term pre-ordained.* (Āl ʿImrān, 3:145)

In other words, therefore, death is a natural phenomenon. Where there is life, death is sure to follow. Moreover, according to the Qur'ānic teaching, the moment of death would be at the time when the soul is separated from the body. But one has to concede that the Qur'ān does not in any way tell us anything about the nature of the soul nor of its location in the human body, hence the dilemma of Muslims insofar as brain death is concerned. Referring specifically to the *rūḥ* (the spirit or soul) the Qur'ān simply states the following:

> *They ask you (O Muḥammad) concerning the* rūḥ *(spirit or soul). Say: The spirit (or soul) is of the authority of my Lord, of knowledge it is only a little that is communicated to you.* (Banī Isrā'īl, 17:85)

Commenting on the above verse, Sayyid Quṭb states in his celebrated *Fī Ẓilāl al-Qur'ān* that man has (through his God-given ingenuity) invented many undreamt-of things and discovered many unheard-of natural phenomena. But he is confused about the soul and remains helpless in solving its mystery in view of the fact that it is beyond the reach/range of human perception. Man is unacquainted with the reality of the soul, its property and nature. He is unaware of its routes of arrival and departure (into and out of the human body). He does not know where it comes from, where it is (located) and where it goes to (upon separation from the body). His knowledge pertaining to the unknown realm is limited to what Allah ﷻ makes known to us through the medium of revelation, i.e. the reality of the soul cannot be discovered through scientific observation, experimentation or speculation.[6]

CHAPTER 15

DELIBERATIONS OF MUSLIM SCHOLARS ON THE END OF HUMAN LIFE

Death of the vast majority of human beings is still being determined by the cessation of heartbeat and respiration. A body that becomes lifeless is in no position to breathe nor can it move. In other words it does not manifest any of the signs of life. However, modern biotechnological innovation has made it possible for patients with head injuries, for example, who are unable to breathe on their own, to do so by means of a ventilator. It is in such cases that the problem of determining the moment of death arises. Muslim scholars have always been concerned about ascertaining the end of human life because of the worldly and religious consequences that follow the pronouncement of death.

I. Consequences Following Death

According to Islamic Law when a person is pronounced dead then certain worldly and religious consequences follow. Some of the worldly consequences are:[1]

- that certain contracts made by the dead person are regarded as valid, while others, such as silent partnerships and the like, become void;
- that any will made by him, up to a maximum limit defined by Islamic Law, becomes effective, and its amount is taken out of his property and added to that of the persons mentioned in the will;
- that his property is no longer his, for it now belongs to his legal heirs;

- that his debts have to be paid, whether they are due or not;
- that the effects of death on securities and promissory notes go into effect;
- that the support he had to pay to certain people is no longer due;
- that his marriage comes to an end, his wife begins her waiting period (*ʿiddah*)[2], and the deferred part of his wife's dowry (*mahr*) is due;
- that whatever objects he is entrusted with for safekeeping must be given back to their owners.

The religious consequences pertain to:

- the washing of the deceased;
- performance of the *ṣalāt al-janāzah* (prayer for the dead);
- burial according to Islamic rites;
- condolences that are to be extended to the deceased's family and relatives.[3]

II. Near Death Signs

Muslim jurists make use of empirical knowledge and cite some signs which signify the approach of death. Ibn Qudāmah, the Ḥanbalī jurist, for example, states in his *al-Mughnī* that death is imminent when the legs (of the dying person) drop down, the jaws separate, the nose becomes crooked, facial skin becomes flabby and temples collapse.[4]

III. Definition of Death

Islam, like the other major religions, subscribes to the view that every human being is a composite of body and spirit or soul. Imām al-Ghazālī in his celebrated *Iḥyā' ʿUlūm al-Dīn* points out that the body has been constituted in such a manner as to accommodate the soul and that death is the separation of the soul from the body.[5] At this juncture, three pertinent questions need to be addressed and they are related to the role of the spirit or soul within the body, the locus of the soul and the moment of death.

A. *Role of the Spirit or Soul*

Qāḍī Mujāhid al-Islām Qāsimī of the Islamic Fiqh Academy of India, explains that in view of the fact that Allah ﷻ has stated in the Qur'ān (17:85) that He is the One Who has knowledge of the *rūḥ* (spirit or soul), some scholars are of the opinion that it is not permissible to discuss the nature of the soul, while others maintain that it is permissible to do so.[6] Thus the soul has been described by some scholars as follows:

> The spirit or soul is a luminous, high, living and mobile object and differs in its nature from the physical body. It gets into the essence of the organs and penetrates them the same way as water penetrates the rose .... When the physical body is ready to receive it, it gives that body life and all that comes with life....[7]

Imām al-Ghazālī describes the role of the soul in the following manner:

> It is by means of the soul that man is the master of creation as it is by means of the soul that man acquires the knowledge of Allah and His attributes and not through any other organ of the body. It is by means of the soul that man can attain nearness to Allah and makes the necessary effort to realize Him. So the soul is the king of the body and the body's different organs are its servants and carry out its orders and commands.[8]

Dr Muḥammad Naʿīm Yāsīn of the College of Islamic Law and Islamic Studies, University of Kuwait, points out that Muslim scholars are of the view that every voluntary activity performed by man is conditioned by the spirit or soul. Thus when someone dies, the soul ceases to exercise any control over the body, resulting in the absence of voluntary movement within the body. Spontaneous or compulsory motion which may be termed as cellular life, i.e. that form of life over which the individual has no control, does not fall within the domain of the effect of the spirit or soul. In other words, such a life persists without the existence of the spirit or soul within the body. At the most, therefore, it may be plausible to hold that the form of life (after the soul departs the body) is that which Allah ﷻ, the Most Powerful and Sublime, creates within the body before the spirit or soul is breathed into it.[9]

Commenting on the Qur'ānic verse *'every soul is bound to taste death'* (Āl ʿImrān, 3:185), the Muslim philosopher, Fakhr al-Dīn al-Rāzī (1150–1209) points out that the soul does not die with the body. This is so because in order to be in a position to taste something, an aspect of that creature has to be alive at the moment of tasting, and thus the implied meaning of the above verse is that every soul will taste the death of the body.[10]

B. *Locus of the Soul*

Medical science tells us that the brain is the centre of human activity, while Muslim scholars are of the view that the organs carry out the dictates of the soul. Qāḍī Mujāhid al-Islām Qāsimī explains that there is no contradiction between the two viewpoints. He points out that medical science concerns itself with the brain because the soul, which is a non-rational entity, is beyond its scope. He then states that the soul makes the brain stem the centre through which it functions.[11] Dr Muḥammad Naʿīm Yāsīn renforces this view by stating that it would be hard to believe that mere movements performed by the organs through instructions received from the brain could produce a feeling of pain, pleasure, joy, reassurance or other states attainable by man.[12] According to him, therefore, it is the soul or spirit which controls the living body through the brain. Moreover, Dr Yāsīn substantiates his stance by arguing that if the brain is responsible for every voluntary action of the body organs, the brain's own action cannot be attributed to the mere material, tangible cells of the brain because abstract and immaterial things cannot be produced by a material entity without the intervention of another source. This source, therefore, is a rational, living, non-material and intangible existence, namely the soul, which stands behind every rational activity carried out by the brain.[13] Here, a Qur'ānic reference which affirms that the soul will be held responsible for its actions on this earth may be cited:

> *Every soul will be (held) in pledge for its deeds.* (al-Muddaththir, 74:38)

From this one may rightly deduce that in *al-Ākhirah* (life after death), it is the soul and not the brain that will enjoy the blessings of *al-Jannah* (Paradise) or suffer the punishment in *al-Jahannam* (Hell).

C. *The Moment of Death*

Imām al-Ghazālī explains that death occurs at the moment when the soul is separated from the body and that at this juncture, the body ceases to be an instrument of the soul.[14] Muslim jurists in general uphold the traditional definition of clinical death which is permanent cessation of heartbeat and respiration. However, as pointed out earlier, advances made in the field of biomedical technology have complicated the issue of determining the moment of death. The mechanical ventilator, for example, can help to keep the organs of the person diagnosed brain dead perfused with blood in order that these organs remain viable for transplantation. The issue of the moment of death is not regarded by Muslims as an amoral one, to them it poses a real moral dilemma. In view of the fact that the Qur'ān and the *Sunnah* are silent on this issue, there are differences of opinion among contemporary Muslim scholars on the issue of brain stem death.

Muslim physician Dr Aḥmad Shawqī Ibrāhīm, a consultant in Internal Diseases, Al-Ṣabāḥ Hospital, Kuwait, and Dr Aḥmad al-Qāḍī of the Akbar Clinic, Panama City, Florida, USA, hold the view that the person whose brain stem has died may be pronounced dead.[15] On the other hand, there are Muslim physicians like Dr Hassan Hathout, a former member of staff of the Faculty of Medicine, University of Kuwait, and now residing in the USA, who is cautious about pronouncing death upon a person whose brain stem has died. He is of the view that, with the progress being made in the field of medical science, it may well be possible, in the near or distant future, to save the life of such a person.[16]

Muslim jurist Qāḍī Mujāhid al-Islām Qāsimī states that once the brain stem dies, the soul leaves the body.[17] Likewise, Dr Yāsīn is of the opinion that if damage to the brain is severe and it (the brain) fails to respond to the soul's will and all other organs irrevocably fail, then the soul departs from the body by the will of Allah ﷻ.[18] There are other Muslim religious scholars who hold the view that it would not be in order to deem a person dead who has been diagnosed brain dead and base their stance on the following Islamic juridical principles:

i. what is known to be certain cannot be cancelled on the basis of what is suspected;
ii. the natural thing is for what has been to go on until a change is proved to have taken place.[19]

Principle (ii) can be substantiated in the following statement of Imām al-Nawawī who suggests that death must be ascertained beyond any doubt:

> If there is suspicion of something unnatural about the death of a person, or if there is the possibility that it is a temporary failure, or if his face reveals signs of terror or something similar suggesting the possibility that he has fainted or that he is in a coma, or the like, (his burial) must be postponed until death is ascertained through the change of odour or something of that sort.[20]

The Religious Rulings Committee, Kuwait Ministry of Endowment, Kuwait, resolved on 14 December, 1981 that a person cannot be considered dead when his brain has died as long as his respiration and circulation systems are alive, even if that life continues through mechanical aid.[21] Shaykh Badr al-Mutawallī ʿAbd al-Bāsiṭ, *Sharīʿah* adviser, Kuwait Finance House, Kuwait, and ʿAbd al-Qādir ibn Muḥammad al-ʿAmārī, judge, First Court of Islamic Law, Qatar, do not dismiss the probability that in the future Allah ﷻ may inspire some researchers to discover a means to restore life to the brain after it has stopped functioning.[22] Shaykh Muḥammad al-Mukhtār al-Salāmī, the Muftī of Tunisia, is of the view that it would not be right to consider a brain dead person to be dead, as long as the essential systems of such a person are alive.[23]

Here, it may be appropriate to note that the stance of contemporary Muslim scholars who are against endorsing brain stem death as the end of human life is based upon the view of the classical Muslim jurists who, as Dr Tawfīq al-Wā'il points out, never recognized the mind or awareness as the source of life but maintained that it is the body which is involved in determining life and death, because it is the body that actually moves.[24]

CHAPTER 16

ISLAMIC JURIDICAL RESOLUTIONS ON BRAIN STEM DEATH

In this chapter an attempt is made to discuss the resolutions of the various Islamic Juridical bodies and Muslim jurists on the issue of brain stem death so as to shed light on two issues, namely, the permissibility of switching off the ventilator once a Muslim patient is diagnosed as brain stem dead, and the legality of retrieving his/her organs – heart or liver or kidney – for the purpose of transplantation into the body of someone else.

I. Switching Off the Life-support Apparatus

A decade ago, at the conclusion of the Seminar on 'Human Life: Its Inception and End as Viewed by Islam' held at the Kuwait Hilton Hotel (1405 AH/1985), it was resolved that once a human being is ascertained to have reached the stage of brain stem death, that person is to be considered to have withdrawn from life. However, caution was expressed in that additional detailed study ought to be undertaken in order to determine which rulings for the dead would apply immediately upon brain stem death diagnosis and which ones should be postponed until all major systems of the body come to a stop. But, it was agreed that when death of the brain stem is certified by a report of a committee of medical specialists, it would be lawful to remove resuscitation equipment.[1]

The Council of the Islamic Fiqh Academy of the Organization of the Islamic Conference, during its third session held in Amman (1407 AH/1986), resolved that the *Sharīʿah* rules for the dead become applicable upon the following:

i. a person who suffers cardio-respiratory arrest and the physicians confirm that such an arrest is irreversible;
ii. a person whose brain activity has ceased and the physicians confirm that such a cessation is irreversible and that the brain has entered the state of decomposition. Under such circumstances the patient may be weaned off the intensive care equipment even though some organs of his body, like the heart, continue to function artificially with the help of the life-support equipment.[2]

The Council of the Islamic Fiqh Academy of *Rābiṭat al-ʿĀlam al-Islāmī*, during its tenth session held in Makkah (1408 AH/1987), resolved that the patient who is on life-support equipment may be removed from the equipment if three expert physicians confirm that there is no form of brain activity and that damage to his brain is irreversible. However, according to *Sharīʿah* ruling, death will only be pronounced on such a person when respiration and heartbeat finally cease after switching off the equipment.[3]

Although Qāḍī Mujāhid al-Islām Qāsimī holds the view that the soul leaves the body once the brain stem dies, he states in a article dated 29 *Rajab* 1409 AH that Muslim scholars and jurists are still in the process of formulating resolutions on the permissibility of switching off the life-support equipment once the patient is diagnosed as brain stem dead and on other matters pertaining to *Sharīʿah* rulings for the dead that could become applicable on brain stem dead patients.[4]

The late Shaykh Jād al-Ḥaqq was of the view that it would not be sinful for the special medical officer administering treatment to the patient on life-support, to disconnect such cardio-respiratory apparatus which assists breathing and heartbeat, if he was convinced that the patient was dying.[5]

The Majlis al-Shūrā al-Islāmī, Gatesville, Cape Town, South Africa, in a document dated 5 May 1994 states that when those qualified to make judgements on brain death declare such a person dead, then the *Sharīʿah* concurs with this judgement and also regards such a person as dead.[6] However, no mention is made about removing such a patient from the life-support equipment. It may be inferred that the Majlis al-Shūrā al-Islāmī would assent to that.

Shaykh ʿAbd al-Karīm Toffar of the Islamic *Sharīʿah* College, Cape Town, South Africa, endorses the view of the late Shaykh Jād al-Ḥaqq and states, in a document dated *Muḥarram* 1415 (1994), that if a person's nervous system is dead (which includes his brain), his other systems will in due course die and cease to function. It would thus not be permissible to use life-supporting apparatus when nervous system death has occurred. The patient should be allowed to die, and thus any attempt to try to prolong life would be tantamount to punishing the patient.[7]

II. Retrieving Organs from Brain Stem Dead Patients

Muslim scholars are divided on the issue of retrieving organs from brain stem dead patients for transplantation purposes. Some of them cautiously suggest that further research ought to be undertaken in this domain. There are others who favour conditioned permissibility, while others deem it non-permissible, and yet others go a step farther and equate it to an act of murder.

A. *Need for Further Research*

Qāḍī Mujāhid al-Islām Qāsimī[8] and the Muslim Judicial Council, Cape Town, South Africa, concur that further research needs to be undertaken on the issue of removing organs from brain stem dead patients for transplantation purposes.[9]

B. *Conditional Permissibility*

The Council of the Islamic Fiqh Academy of the Organization of the Islamic Conference during its fourth session held in Jeddah (February 1988), resolved that it is permissible to transplant the organ from a dead person to a living recipient on the condition that it has been authorized by the deceased or by his heirs after his death. The Council during the same session also noted that death may take two forms:

a. when all functions of the brain come to a complete stop, and no medical cure can reverse the situation;
b. when the heart and respiration come to a stop, and no medical cure can reverse the situation.[10]

From the above, it may be implied, although not categorically stated, that it is permissible to retrieve organs from brain stem dead patients for transplantation purposes.

Dr Muṣṭafā Ṣabrī Ardughdu of Marmara College of Divinities, Istanbul, Turkey, is of the view that if a just and trustworthy Muslim doctor is certain that the person whose heart or eye are to be removed is going to die soon[11] and has no doubt about that, it would then be lawful to transplant his organ to another person who is in need of it. He bases his stance on the juridical principle which maintains that the right of the living supersedes consideration over that of the dead.[12]

Shaykh Muḥammad al-Mukhtār al-Salāmī, the Muftī of Tunisia, states that if a person is living only with the aid of resuscitation equipment, it is lawful to use his organ to save the life of another. He even stipulates that family members of such a person from whose body the organ is removed may waive their right to blood money.[13] This implies that engaging in such a procedure is not to be regarded as a crime.

C. *Non-Permissibility*

In the recommendations adopted at the conclusion of the Seminar on 'Human Life: Its Inception and End as Viewed by Islam', Kuwait, 1985, no mention was made of the permissibility of retrieving organs from brain stem dead patients, hence it remains an unresolved issue. Likewise, since the Council of the Islamic Fiqh Academy of *Rābiṭat al-ʿĀlam al-Islāmī*, during its tenth session (1987), resolved that a person who is diagnosed as brain dead can only be pronounced dead when respiration and heartbeat cease after switching off the life-support equipment, it *ipso facto* implies that retrieving organs from brain stem dead patients is not permissible within the dictates of the *Sharīʿah*.[14]

The Muslim Judicial Council, Cape Town, South Africa, subscribes to the view that a person placed on the ventilator whose heartbeat, circulation and breathing are being kept going artificially is to be considered as being alive.[15] From this, it can be deduced that the Muslim Judicial Council is inclined towards the view that it would not be permissible to retrieve organs from brain stem dead patients.

D. *Tantamount to Murder*

In a document issued by the Majlis al-ʿUlamā', Port Elizabeth, South Africa, dated 14 February 1994, it is stated that removing any organs from a person pronounced brain dead entails two major crimes, namely, the perpetration of murder and the unlawful act of misappropriating his organs.[16]

CHAPTER 17

EUTHANASIA

The word euthanasia comes from the Greek *euthanatos* derived from the words *eu* and *thanatos*, meaning 'good' and 'death' respectively.[1] Therefore, euthanasia means allowing an easy and good death. It is also defined as 'mercy killing' of the hopelessly ill, injured or incapacitated and the ending of the life, as painlessly as possible, of the patient who is suffering from a terminal illness and is undergoing extreme pain. Euthanasia thus includes:

- death by administering drugs with or without the patient's explicit request;
- a decision to withhold or withdraw potentially life-prolonging treatment so as to hasten the patient's death;
- alleviating pain with large doses of opioids, allowing for a probability of causing death, but not explicitly intending to cause death;
- administering to the patient an overdose of barbiturates or a lethal injection with the aim of terminating the life of the patient.

Euthanasia is in essence the termination of the life of the terminally ill at their request or in their interest. Euthanasia continues to pose a religious, legal and moral problem in all cultural and religious traditions. Before tackling the issue of euthanasia in the light of the *Sharīʿah*, it is imperative that we deliberate upon Islam's attitude to the sanctity of life.

I. Sanctity of Life

Islam like other religions upholds the sanctity of life as mentioned in the Qur'ānic verse (5:32) quoted earlier. However, it should be noted that the Islamic penal code based on Divine injunctions, advocates the death penalty for those who commit certain grave crimes. It is for the sake of curtailing crime and ensuring peace, security and tranquillity that Islam prescribes preventive measures and just punishments for acts that tend towards terminating life without reasonable justification.[2] The Qur'ān stipulates the death penalty for wilful murder:

> *O you who believe! Just retribution is ordained for you in respect of the murdered...* (al-Baqarah, 2:178)

The Arabic equivalent for the punishment of the person guilty of committing murder is *al-qiṣāṣ* (just retribution). This measure ensures that if the death sentence is to be carried out then only the one guilty of the crime will lose his/her life. However, it needs to be pointed out here that the family of the one who has been murdered also has other options: either to forgive the murderer, or to accept compensation.[3]

II. Active and/or Involuntary Euthanasia

Active euthanasia is the deliberate act undertaken by the attending physician to cause the death of his/her patient, while involuntary euthanasia involves ending the patient's life without his/her explicit approval. This is carried out on the basis of a paternalistic decision to do what is best for the terminally ill. It ought to be pointed out here that the Qur'ān warns:

> *And do not take any human being's life – (the life) which Allah has made sacred save with right (justice).* (Banī Isrā'īl, 17:33)

It is evident from this verse that human life is sacred and therefore cannot be disposed of except for a just cause, that is, in execution of a legal sentence, or in a just war, or in legitimate self-defence.[4] To terminate the life of the terminally ill does not fall within the ambit of 'a just cause'. Therefore if a medical practitioner were to deliberately end the life of his/her patient then he/she would be guilty of homicide. Life and death are the prerogatives of Allah ﷻ as categorically stated in the Qur'ān:

> *Allah gives life and death, and Allah sees well all that you do.* (Āl ʿImrān, 3:156)

One may safely infer from this verse that even if the physician chooses to increase the dose of the medication, being fully aware that that would in effect cause death, he would then be held liable for terminating the life of his/her patient which equates to murder under the *Sharīʿah*. While it is true that intention (*niyyah*) of the physician is beyond the jurisdiction of the judge or the court of law, yet his/her intention cannot escape the ever-watchful supervision of Allah ﷻ. The Qur'ān states the following in this regard:

> *He (Allah) knows the treachery of the eyes and what the hearts conceal.* (al-Mu'min, 40:19)

Hence, although the physician may not be convicted by the court of the land, he/she would nevertheless be answerable to Allah ﷻ for his/her part in terminating the life of the terminally ill.

III. Voluntary Euthanasia

In the event that a terminally ill patient requests the attending physician to terminate his/her life as a result of his/her excruciating pain and suffering, then such a request would be termed voluntary euthanasia or assisted suicide. The Qur'ān explicitly censures such an action and categorically states:

> *Do not kill yourselves: for verily Allah is to you Most Merciful.* (al-Nisā', 4:29)

Suicide, self-inflicted or assisted, is a crime according to the *Sharīʿah* and hence constitutes a sin in the sight of Allah ﷻ. The following *ḥadīth* discloses the fate of a person who terminates his/her life:

> There was a man before you who was wounded. The pain became unbearable and so he took a knife and cut off his hand. Blood began to ooze out profusely leading to his death. Almighty Allah said: 'My servant hastened himself to Me and so I made Paradise unlawful for him.'[5]

From this *ḥadīth* we gather that while voluntary euthanasia may apparently end the terminally ill's pain and suffering in this world, his/her problem would be further compounded in the life Hereafter by being excluded from inheriting a place in Paradise. At this juncture, it is necessary to understand the Muslim attitude towards pain and suffering.

IV. The Concept of Pain and Suffering

According to the Islamic philosophy of life, there is a transcendental dimension to pain and suffering. The Qur'ān tells us that those who claim to believe in Allah ﷻ will not be left alone after proclamation of their belief (*īmān*):

> *Do people reckon that they will be left (in ease) after saying 'We believe', and (that) they will not be tried with affliction?* (al-ʿAnkabūt, 29:2)

The Qur'ān further asserts that the believers will be put to the test in various ways:

> *Be sure that We shall test you with something of fear and hunger, some loss in goods or lives or the fruits of your toil, but give glad tidings to those who patiently persevere, who say when afflicted with calamity: 'To Allah we belong and to Him is our return.' They are the ones on whom (descend) blessings from Allah, and mercy, and they are the ones that are guided.* (al-Baqarah, 2:155–7)

Thus we find that Muslims in general view affliction with a disease, fatal or otherwise, as a test of their faith and true resignation to their Creator. In fact, such tribulation contributes in their favour in that it helps to expiate their minor sins. This is evident from the following *ḥadīth*:

> When a Muslim is tried with a disease in his body it is said to the angel: Write for him the good actions which he used to do. If He (Allah) cures him, He absolves him (of all sins); and if He takes his life (as a result of this disease), He forgives him and shows mercy upon him.[6]

There is, therefore, no justification for ending the life of a person so as to relieve him/her of suffering. The Qur'ān clearly states:

> *Allah does not tax any soul beyond that which it can bear.* (al-Baqarah, 2:286)

Muslims believe in the Hereafter, the real and everlasting life, and it is this belief which enables them to bear their pain and suffering with what the Qur'ān terms *ṣabr* (perseverance).

VI. Passive Euthanasia

Passive euthanasia is an omission on the part of the attending physician to, for example, resuscitate the terminally ill which results in his/her death. In this context, the physician would be absolved of liability in causing the death of the patient on the basis of the Islamic legal principle of *lā ḍarar wa lā ḍirār* (no harm and no harassment). This principle justifies one to allow death to take its natural course. Moreover, it ought to be pointed out here that while the physician is obligated to provide medical care at all times, treatment may be discontinued if in his/her opinion, as a member of *ahl al-khibrah* (experts in the field of medicine), there is little or no hope of the patient's recovery. The same argument would justify the non-utilization of nasogastric tubal feeding if recourse to such form of artificial feeding would, according to medical experts, not benefit the patient. Likewise, it would be permissible for the attending physician to switch off the life-support equipment, once his/

her patient has been diagnosed as brain stem dead and medical experts have confirmed that cessation of the patient's brain activity is irreversible.[7]

VII. Motivations for Euthanasia

Advocates of euthanasia justify their stance on the basis of the following:

a. economic factors
b. considerations of hospital space, beds, staff and therapeutic equipment that could otherwise be utilized by other patients;
c. death with dignity.

Let us now examine each of these motivations so as to ascertain their validity in the light of Islamic teachings.

A. *Economic Factors*

As a student in America, I noticed that people there were afraid of falling ill in view of the high cost of medical care. It always baffled me as to how this great nation that reached the moon was unable to solve the problem of reducing the extremely high cost of medical care. The situation in South Africa is not very different. People tend to become more sick when they learn of the high cost or medicine and medical care. Economic factors are of no consideration in Islam's censuring of euthanasia. In a Muslim state it is the responsibility of the executive head, whether Caliph or King, President or Prime Minister, to secure funds from the *Bayt al-Māl* (Public Treasury) in order to assist the needy in meeting their medical expenses or other needs. Islam has left a rich legacy in this regard and Muslim rulers are known to have taken a personal interest in alleviating the suffering of the sick. For example, in the Manṣūrī Hospital in Cairo, built by the Mamlūk ruler, al-Manṣūr Sayf al-Dīn Qalā'ūn in 1284, everyone was treated without financial cost to the patient.[8]

B. *Considerations of Hospital Space, Beds, Staff and Therapeutic Devices*

The argument for justifying euthanasia in these instances is centred upon the logic of preference given to one individual over another on the basis of the quality of life. This proposition would seem plausible if it were related to a terminally ill patient in comparison with another younger patient who had a better prognosis. However, for a Muslim, the problem becomes acute when faced with the issue of opting for one life at the expense of another. This is so because the Qur'ān emphatically states that death comes about only by Allah's will:

> *And no human being can die save by Allah's leave, at a term pre-ordained.* (Āl ʿImrān, 3:145)

Thus there is no guarantee that a patient who is not suffering from a fatal disease will outlive one who is terminally ill. Both are equally important members of the human race. The solution is certainly not to get rid of one (the terminally ill patient, for instance) in order to accommodate the other. The answer to this problem perhaps is to allocate more funds in order to increase hospital space so that more beds may be made available, more staff may be employed and more therapeutic devices may be procured.

C. *Death with Dignity*

The concept of death with dignity is what gave birth to the hospice movement in England. Terminally ill patients who are admitted to hospices worldwide are given the opportunity to live with dignity and to die with dignity. This means that the dying patients are made to participate as far as possible in enjoying what they would like to enjoy rather than being confined to their beds. Moreover, pain-killers are administered to them so as to relieve their suffering because it is felt that if pain is not controlled, then it robs them of dignity. According to Professor Christiaan Barnard, who pioneered open-heart surgery, suffering causes a patient to become depersonalized. In fact, both he and

Dr Marius Barnard (his brother) have vowed to help each other in the event that either found himself in circumstances that would 'justify' euthanasia. This 'could be done either with the administration of a fatal overdose if the sufferer was incapable of helping himself, or by leaving within reach enough tablets so that the sufferer could take his own life.'[9] This would be a case of assisted suicide and suicide (assisted or self-inflicted), as has been explained above, is a sin in Islam. The suffering which one undergoes as a result of any disease does not rob one of one's dignity, but rather benefits one spiritually as can be deduced from the following *ḥadīth*:

> ʿAbd Allāh ibn Masʿūd (may Allah be pleased with him) reports that: I visited the Prophet ﷺ while he was having high fever. I touched him with my hand and said, 'O Allah's Messenger ﷺ! You have a high fever.' Allah's Messenger ﷺ said, 'Yes, I have so much fever the equivalent of what two men among you may have.' I said, 'Is it because you will have a double reward.' Allah's Messenger ﷺ said, 'Yes. No Muslim is afflicted with harm because of sickness or some inconvenience, but that Allah will remove his sins for him as a tree sheds its leaves.'[10]

Moreover, according to Anas ibn Mālik the Prophet ﷺ gave them the following advice:

> None of you should wish for death because of a calamity befalling him; but if he has to wish for death he should say: 'O Allah! Keep me alive as long as life is better for me and let me die if death is better for me.'[11]

A Muslim should therefore place his/her trust (*tawakkul*) at all times in Allah ﷻ and despair must not be allowed to set in during adverse times. While accepting the eventuality of death one may not lose hope of the Mercy of Allah ﷻ:

> *Do not lose heart nor grieve for you must gain mastery if you are true in faith.* (Āl ʿImrān, 3:139)

CONCLUSION

Notwithstanding the fact that the different types of organ transplantation are aimed at improving the quality of life, such procedures are perceived differently in the Islamic world. Muslims follow the *Sharīʿah* (the Revealed Law) and therefore ask whether the *Sharīʿah* sanctions it. Since the *Sharīʿah* is silent on this issue, one seeks guidance from the science of Islamic jurisprudence (*al-Fiqh*) and its ruling of *ijtihād*. It is on this basis that its permissibility may be argued on the ground of 'necessity' (*al-ḍarūrah*) i.e. necessary for the betterment and preservation of human and animal life. However, as pointed out in the relevant chapters, there are certain broad juridical principles which can in reality be advanced to restrict this permissibility.

In recent years there has been a renewed call by the 'Animal Rights' movement against the use of animals aimed at new discoveries or for testing the safety of medical and household products. It must be conceded, however, that there are valid reasons both for and against animal experimentation. The thalidomide disaster in Britain in the early 1960s was indeed a terrible tragedy. More than 10,000 babies were born with stumped or missing limbs. This reality proved that animals react differently to humans. In other words, therefore, animal experimentation can at times mislead science and endanger human life. On the other hand, one may rightly argue that both animals and humans have benefitted as a result of biomedical investigations. For example, diabetic investigations carried out on dogs resulted in benefitting both the diabetic patients and dogs in view of the fact that insulin came to be used in veterinary practice to control canine diabetes.

While the rule of necessity may be used to justify animal experimentation, it nevertheless behoves the scientists not to subject animals to any form of unnecessary, indiscriminate or painful experimentation. It is therefore essential that every effort be made to substitute animals wherever possible with non-sentient systems.

As regards animal tissues and organs for human use, the permissibility is deduced from the juridical principle 'when two interests conflict, give preference to that which will 'anticipate greater benefit'. However, it is imperative that this permissibility be hedged by the following conditions:

i. No alternative substitutes to animal tissues or organs are available, e.g. synthetic parts;
ii. that animal to man transplant is the only means possible to save human life;
iii. that the expected degree of success is relatively high.

There appears to be no limit as to what mankind can accomplish in its scientific and technological pursuits. However, it is imperative that mankind comes to terms with the fact that although it has the ability to manipulate nature, utmost restraint should be exercised. Lamenting on human nature, the famous Muslim physician/philosopher Abū Yūsuf Yaʿqūb ibn Isḥāq al-Kindī (d. 259 AH/873) exclaimed: 'All Allah's creation, the animals and beasts of the fields and forests and the fish of the sea, are satisfied and happy with what they have. But man is not.'[1]

On the issue of animal experimentation, therefore, let human beings take heed that in the pursuit of scientific endeavour they are not blinded by self-indulgence, but rather endeavour to specifically alleviate human and animal suffering.

As far as blood transfusion is concerned, Muslim scholars concur that Muslims may resort to blood transfusion in life-threatening situations. This in no way suggests that Muslims have committed their faith absolutely to modern science at the expense of their belief in Allah ﷻ as the Ultimate Healer. It must, in this context, be understood that failing to attempt to save human lives, even if this is by means of blood transfusion, would be in direct violation of the Qur'ānic imperative (5:32) to save lives.

Muslims are well aware of the *ḥadīth*: 'For every disease there is a cure'[2] and therefore view blood transfusion as a type of cure in cases of blood loss and other blood-related disorders or diseases.

The deliberations of the respective Muslim jurists, cited in Chapter 7, undoubtedly serve to enlighten the reader on the Islamic stand on blood transfusion; however, certain observations need to be noted.

Muftī Shafī' in order to emphasize that blood is *najas* (impure) quotes a juristic opinion of Imām al-Shāfi'ī which may have been intended to caution against the amateurish insertion of blood under the skin (resulting in the forming of a type of lump), and is not strictly pertinent to the issue of blood transfusion itself. In contemporary practice, the removal of the newly-transfused blood is impossible. Therefore, in the light of this it may be asked: If blood is to be regarded as unclean, not for consumption but absolutely for transfusion, must the blood-recipient be regarded as perpetually unclean and hence in no position to offer the daily *ṣalāh* (obligatory prayers)?

Moreover, in according permission for blood transfusion (in extraordinary circumstances) the analogy the Muftī draws between blood and milk is questionable since milk and blood are physiologically and anatomically different from each other in several ways. Firstly, milk is produced by the mammary gland whilst the constituents of blood, i.e. the red and white cells and platelets are formed in the bone marrow. Secondly, milk is specific to the adult female, in the gestational and lactation periods, and is localized to the breasts while blood permeates each and every organ of the body Thirdly, the functional aspect of breast milk is nutritional and serves to protect the infant from susceptibility to infection (especially in the first six months after birth). The function of blood on the other hand is manifold. It can be said to be a vehicle supplying oxygen and other substances, absorbed from the gastrointestinal tract, to the tissues and returning carbon dioxide and metabolized products to lungs and kidneys respectively. Overall, blood serves the purpose of sustaining life. Its white cells protect the body from infection.[3]

Shaykh Aḥmad's view that the State may encourage potential donors of blood by offering them payment in return for this service, indirectly suggests that he opts in favour of the fringe benefit for the voluntary donor. It would be more appropriate for the potential donors to regard their service as a *ṣadaqah* (charity) for the primary concern for the well-being of fellow human beings rather than any 'fringe benefits' arising therefrom. His statement that the money given to them by the State be utilized for foodstuff in order to replenish their lost energies, has no medical justification.

Regarding the religious factor in blood transfusion, Muftī Shafīʿs view is conditioned by the analogy between milk and blood. This may have caused him to forget to caution Muslims against their blood being mingled with that of non-Muslims which may be 'polluted' with food and drink (e.g. pork and alcohol) that are expressly forbidden to Muslims.

It would be appropriate here to reiterate that the permissibility for resorting to blood transfusion is governed by the juristic principle, viz. 'necessity renders the forbidden permissible'. Thus in the event of there being an available substitute to blood this permissibility would then, *ipso facto*, be regarded as inapplicable.

As for transplantation of human limbs, it was pointed out that Muslim scholars differ on this issue. Following the establishment of Islamic Fiqh Academies in various parts of the Muslim world there is at present consensus that Muslims may opt for this procedure in order to improve the quality of life. The author of the present work endorses this stance for he strongly feels that organ transplantation, like blood transfusion, is a form of treatment. Hence, Muslims should avail themselves of this form of treatment as long as there is no other alternative. Moreover, consenting to donate one's kidney to either a member of one's family or a friend who is in dire need of it ought to be viewed as an act of sharing motivated by the spirit of love, compassion and sympathy for a fellow human being.

There is agreement among Muslims and the followers of other traditions that the dead human body must be treated with utmost respect. This may lead one to regard cadaveric transplantation as mutilation. However, one ought to note that justification for

Muslims to derive benefit from such transplantation is governed by the Islamic juridical principle which takes into consideration the interest of man by maintaining that the right of the living supersedes that of the dead.

This brings us to the question as to whether it would be permissible for a Muslim to include organ donation in his/her last will and testament. One of the arguments put forward against the validity of such inclusion is the notion that a price cannot be set for human organs/limbs. This consideration would be relevant if the testator were to stipulate a price for the use of his/her organ after his/her demise. As for the other objection which relates to the fact that a person may not give away that which he/she does not own, it must be pointed out that every Muslim accepts that everything belongs to Allah ﷻ. However, no one can deny that every person has been given partial if not full ownership, over whatever he/she disposes. Therefore, incorporating organ donation in one's will for the purpose of saving another life or enhancing it can in no way be termed as *khiyānah fī al-amānah* (breach of trust). After all, this gesture is motivated by the *niyyah* (intention) to assist a person in need. Thus although such a stipulation in one's last will and testament may not in effect conform to the strict dictates of the *Sharīʿah*, the author of the present work is inclined to hold that it would at least be morally binding on the part of the heirs to execute such a direction.

Insofar as human cloning is concerned, Muslim religious scholars have unanimously issued a *fatwā* (religious decree) against research in the field of human cloning. It would not be justified for Muslims to derive benefit from therapeutic uses of human cloning in view of the fact that the evils that will accrue from it will far outweigh any good. Furthermore, although human cloning technology may fulfil the dreams of infertile couples, it has been pointed out that procreating the human race through this form of technological manipulation is not only morally and ethically unjustifiable in most major religions, it also undermines the institution of marriage and impacts negatively upon the Islamic law of inheritance.

Diagnosis of brain stem death is relevant to the issue of retrieving vital organs, viz. heart, lung, liver and kidney for transplantation purposes. In this regard, David Lamb points out that 'the most suitable cadaveric donors are brain stem dead individuals who have died in intensive care units.'[4]

At this juncture, it may be appropriate to question as to whether it would be an act of murder to retrieve a vital organ from a brain stem dead patient for transplantation purposes? Dr Muḥammad Sulaymān al-Ashqar, an expert in the field of Islamic jurisprudence, Kuwait, argues that a brain stem dead person should be considered to be virtually dead and is to be treated as dead as far as permissibility to disconnect the resuscitation equipment or to remove his organ for transplantation purposes is concerned.[5] In other words, he likens brain stem death to the attainment of unstable life. Muslim jurists hold unstable life to be the stage immediately before the body becomes lifeless, i.e. the process of spirit or soul departure.[6] During this stage, the person has no eyesight, is unable to talk and cannot engage in voluntary motion.[7] Dr ʿAbdullāh Muḥammad ʿAbdullāh, counsellor, Higher Court of Appeal, Kuwait, points out that scholars belonging to the *Shāfiʿī* school of Islamic jurisprudence are of the view that if a murderer has caused his victim to reach the stage of unstable life, which is also termed as the stage of the slaughtered or slain, and then another criminal attacks the same victim, then only the first criminal will be punished for murder, while the second criminal will be chastized for violating the sanctity of the dead.[8]

Morever, does the physician's act in retrieving organs from the dead for transplantation purposes constitute violation of the sanctity of the dead? The Council of the Islamic Fiqh Academy of the Organization of the Islamic Conference resolved, during its fourth session held in Jeddah (1408 AH/1988), that it is allowed to transplant an organ from a dead person, if it is essential to keep the beneficiary alive, or if it will assist in restoring a basic function of the beneficiary's body, provided it has been authorized by the deceased or by his heirs after his death or with the permission of the concerned authorities if the deceased has not been identified or has no heirs.[9]

In order to allay fears that retrieving organs from brain stem dead patients would not constitute an act of murder, attention is drawn to the recommendation made at the conclusion of the Seminar on 'Human Life: Its Inception and End of Life as Viewed by Islam' (Kuwait, January 1985), which categorically states: 'Fiqh scholars are inclined to the view that when it is ascertained that a human being has reached the stage of brain stem death, he is considered to have withdrawn from life...'[10]

Euthanasia, as has been pointed out, is a crime in Islam since it is undoubtedly a deliberate attempt to hasten the death of a person. Thus, under Islamic Law, the one who assists a person to end his/her life, like Dr Jack Kevorkian, an American pathologist who has been involved in assisting terminally ill patients to end their lives through inhaling poisonous carbon monoxide, would be guilty of murder. The prerogative to bestow and terminate life according to all Divine religions rests with God. We have seen that the *Sharīʿah* does stipulate the termination of human life as punishment for certain specific crimes. However, such a measure is meted out in the event of violation of the sanctity of God's laws serving as a deterrent for the sake of ensuring peace and protection within society.

Euthanasia is a form of escape for the sufferer. At the same time, it is a means of expediency for the one who administers it. To seek to terminate life on account of economic pressures reflects a sense of irresponsibility on the part of the State and society. Relaxing the laws in order to legalize euthanasia could eventually lead to justifying the termination of the lives of the handicapped and the aged who are often regarded as burdens to their families and to society in general. Legalizing euthanasia will also stifle research aimed at finding cures for many of the sicknesses that are currently regarded as incurable. It ought to be noted here that the Islamic juridical principle *lā ḍarar wa-lā ḍirār* (no harm and no harassment) justifies one in not opting for over-zealous treatment so as to allow death to take its natural course. The aim is not to hasten death, but to refrain from harassing the patient. However, 'palliative' care of the terminally ill in the sense of maintaining basic hygiene and basic nutrition should not be discontinued.

NOTES

Introduction

1. See Muhammad Asad, *The Message of the Qur'ān,* (Gibraltar: Dar al-Andalus Limited, 1980), p. 405, n. 79.
2. Jeff E. Zhorne, 'Organ Transplants: How Far Dare We Go?' in the *Plain Truth* (Cape Town: Ambassador College Agency, September 1985), p. 10.
3. Abū Dāwūd Sulaymān ibn al-Ashʿath al-Sijistānī, *Sunan Abī Dāwūd,* (Beirut: Dār Iḥyā' al-Sunnah al-Nabawiyyah, n.d.), 'Kitāb al-Khātim', ḥadīth no. 4232, vol. 2, p. 92.
4. Zhorne, 'Organ Transplants: How Far Dare We Go?', p. 11.
5. Christiaan N. Barnard, 'Reflections On the First Heart Transplant' in the *South African Medical Journal,* (Pinelands: Publications Division of the Medical Association of South Africa, 5 December 1987), 72 (11), p. xx.
6. M.F.A. Woodruff, 'The Ethics of Organ Transplantation' in *Biology and Ethics* (Proceedings of a Symposium held at the Royal Geographical Society, London on 26–7 September 1968) ed. E.J. Ebling, (London: Academic Press, 1969), pp. 86–9.
7. See 'Pig to Man Transplants: It's Possible – UK Surgeon' in the *Daily News,* (Durban) 1 August, 1988.
8. *Ibid.*

Chapter I

1. *The New Universal Encyclopaedia, (*London: The Amalgamated Press Ltd., n.d.), vol. 14, p. 8402.
2. *Chambers's Encyclopaedia*, (London: George Newnes Ltd., 1959 edn.), vol. 14, p. 355.
3. Munawar A. Anees (ed.), *Health Sciences in Early Islam,* (Texas: Noor Health Foundation/Zahra Publications, 1983), vol. 1, p. 54.
4. *Encyclopaedia Britannica,* (London: Encyclopaedia Britannica Inc., 1971), vol. 23, p. 337.
5. *Chambers's Encyclopaedia*, p. 355.
6. Christiaan N. Barnard, 'Reflections on the First Heart Transplant', p. xx.
7. *Chambers's Encyclopaedia*, p. 355.
8. Anees (ed.), *Health Sciences in Early Islam*, vol. 1, pp. 118–21.

9. Jenny Remfry, 'Ethical Aspects of Animal Experimentation' in *Laboratory Animals: An Introduction for New Experiments*, ed. A.A. Tuffery, (London: John Wiley & Sons Ltd, 1987), p. 8.
10. *Ibid.*, p. 9.
11. *Ibid.*
12. *Ibid.*, p. 10.
13. *Ibid.*, pp. 10–11.

Chapter 2

1. Muḥammad Fazlur Raḥmān Anṣārī, *The Qur'ānic Foundations and Structure of Muslim Society,* (Karachi: Trade and Industry Publications Ltd., 1973), vol. 2, p. 126.
2. Muḥyī al-Dīn Abū Zakariyyā Yaḥyā ibn Sharaf al-Nawawī, *Riyāḍ al-Ṣāliḥīn,* (Lahore: Idārat al-Sunnah, 1398 AH/1978), p. 330.
3. Muslim ibn al-Ḥajjāj al-Naysābūrī, *Ṣaḥīḥ Muslim,* (Cairo: Dār al-Shaʿb, n.d.), 'Kitāb al-Imārah', ḥadīth no. 174, vol. 4, p. 585.
4. James Robson, *Mishkāt al-Maṣābīḥ*, English translation, (Lahore: Sh. Muḥammad Ashraf, May 1964), Bk. 18, 'Jihād', vol. 3, p. 829.
5. Abū Dāwūd al-Sijistānī, *Sunan Abī Dāwūd,* 'Kitāb al-Jihād', ḥadīth no. 2567, vol. 3, p. 27.
6. Al-Ḥāfiẓ B.A. Maṣrī, *Animals in Islam*, (Petersfield: The Athene Trust, 1989), p. 28.
7. Abū ʿAbd al-Raḥmān Aḥmad ibn Shuʿayb al-Nasā'ī, *Sunan al-Nasā'ī,* (Cairo: al-Maktabah al-Tājiriyyah, 1398 AH/1938), 'Kitāb al-Ṣayd wa al-Dhabā'iḥ', vol. 7, p. 207.
8. M.H.K. Sherwani, *Ḥaḍrat Abū Bakr, the First Caliph of Islam*, (trans. by S.M. Haq; Lahore: Sh. Muḥammad Ashraf, 1959), pp. 60–1.
9. Abū ʿĪsā Muḥammad ibn Sawrah al-Tirmidhī, *Sunan al-Tirmidhī*, (Al-Madīnah al-Munawwarah: al-Maktabah al-Salafiyyah,1394 AH/1974), *Abwāb al-Birr wa al-Ṣilah*, vol. 3, p. 217.
10. Muḥammad ibn Ismāʿīl al-Bukhārī, *Ṣaḥīḥ al-Bukhārī*, (Cairo: Dār al-Shaʿb, n.d.), 'Kitāb al-Wakālah', vol. 1, p. 147.
11. *Ibid.*, pp. 146–7.
12. *Sunan al-Tirmidhī*, 'Abwāb al-Jihād', vol. 3, p. 126.
13. *Ṣaḥīḥ al-Bukhārī*, 'Kitāb al-Dhabā'iḥ wa al-Ṣayd', vol. 3, pp. 121–2.
14. *Ṣaḥīḥ Muslim,* 'Kitāb al-Ṣayd wa al-Dhabā'iḥ', ḥadīth no. 54. vol. 4, p. 622.

Chapter 3

1. *Ṣaḥīḥ al-Bukhārī*, 'Kitāb al-Ṭibb', vol. 3, p. 158.
2. Anees (ed.), *Health Sciences in Early Islam*, vol. 1, p. 164.
3. *Ibid.*, vol. 2, p. 66.
4. *Ibid.*, vol. 1, p. 54.

5. Hassan Hathout, *Topics in Islamic Medicine,* (Kuwait: International Organisation of Islamic Medicine, 1st edn., 1984), p. 45.
6. Anees (ed.), *Health Sciences in Early Islam*, vol. 2, p. 197.
7. *Ibid.*, p. 89.
8. Sami K. Hamarneh, 'Al-Birūnī the Father of Islamic Pharmacy and Marine Biology as Demonstrated in As-Saydanah' in Hakim Mohammed Sa'id (ed.), *Al-Birūnī Commemorative Volume,* (Karachi: Hamdard National Foundation, 1979), p. 484.
9. Anees (ed.), *Health Sciences in Early Islam*, vol. 1, p. 56.
10. *Ibid*, vol. 2, p. 138.
11. Hathout, *Topics in Islamic Medicine*, p. 39.
12. Anees (ed.), *Health Sciences in Early Islam*, vol. 2, p. 154.
13. *Ibid.*, vol.1, p. 162.
14. *Ibid.*, vol. 2, p. 169.
15. Hathout, *Topics in Islamic Medicine*, p. 41.

Chapter 4

1. Muḥammad Abū Zahrah, *Uṣūl al-Fiqh,* (Cairo: Dār al-Fikr al-ʿArabī, n.d.), p. 220.
2. *Ibid.*, p. 228.
3. *Ibid.*, p. 301.
4. *Ibid.*, p. 299.
5. Maṣrī, *Animals in Islam*, p. 19.
6. 'Qarār al-Majmaʿ al-Fiqhī bi Sha'n Mawḍūʿ Zirāʿat al-Aʿḍā'' in *Majallat al-Majmaʿ al-Fiqhī*, (Makkah: Rābiṭat al-ʿĀlam al-Islāmī, 1408 AH/1987), p. 40.
7. Islamic Fiqh Academy of India – 'Developing A Religious Law in Modern Times' in *Religion and Law Review*, 1(1) (Summer 1992), p. 178.
8. Jād al-Ḥaqq ʿAlī Jād al-Ḥaqq, *Buḥūth wa Fatāwā Islāmīyyah fī Qaḍāyā Muʿāṣarah,* (Cairo: al-Azhar University, 1994), vol. 3, p. 433.
9. Fayṣal Ibrāhīm Ẓāhir, *Ḥiwār Maʿ Ṭābīb Muslim,* (Cairo: al-Risālah, n.d.), p. 84.
10. Majlis al-ʿUlamā''s document on 'Organ Transplants', unpublished document, p. 3.
11. Yūsuf al-Qaraḍāwī, *Al-Ḥalāl wa al-Ḥarām fī al-Islām*, (Cairo: Maktabah Wahbah, 1400 AH/1980), p. 48.
12. *Ṣaḥīḥ al-Bukhārī,* 'Kitāb al-Ashribah', vol. 3, p. 143.
13. Majlis al-ʿUlamā''s document on Organ Transplants', p. 4.
14. Al-Qaraḍāwī, *Al-Ḥalāl wa al-Ḥarām fī al-Islām*, p. 48.
15. 'Al-Qarār al-Awwal bi Sha'n Mawḍūʿ Zirāʿat al-Aʿḍā'' in *Qarārāt Majlis al-Majmāʿ al-Fiqhī al-Islāmī* (Makkah: Rābiṭat al-ʿĀlam al-Islāmī, 1405 AH/1985), p. 147.
16. Islamic Fiqh Academy of India – 'Developing A Religious Law in Modern Times', p. 178.
17. Ẓāhir, *Ḥiwār Maʿ Ṭābīb Muslim*, p. 84.

Chapter 5

1. Richard M. Titmuss, *The Gift Relationship from Human Blood to Social Policy* (London: George Allen & Unwin Ltd., 1970), p. 15.
2. Afzal Iqbal, *Culture of Islam,* (Lahore: Institute of Islamic Culture, 1974), p. 42.
3. Titmuss, *The Gift Relationship,* p. 15.
4. *Ibid.*, p. 16.
5. *The New International Dictionary of New Testament Theology*, (Exeter: The Paternoster Press Ltd., 1975), vol. 1, p. 221.
6. *Ibid.*, p. 222.
7. Abū al-Walīd Muḥammad Aḥmad Ibn Rushd (al-Qurṭubī), *Bidāyat al-Mujtahid wa Nihāyat al-Muqtaṣid,* (Cairo: Maṭbaʿah Muṣṭafā al-Bābī al-Ḥalabī wa Awlāduh, 1981), vol. 1, p. 34.
8. *Ibid.*
9. For details, see ʿAbd al-Raḥmān al-Jazīrī, *Kitāb al-Fiqh ʿalā al-Madhāhib al-Arbaʿah,* (Beirut: Dār al-Fikr al-ʿArabī, n.d.), vol. 1, p. 133.
10. Al-Qaraḍāwī, *Al-Ḥalāl wa al-Ḥarām fī al-Islām*, pp. 42–3.

Chapter 6

1. Titmuss, *The Gift Relationship*, p. 11.
2. *Ibid.*, p. 12.
3. There are various blood group systems; the ABO system discussed here is only one of them. See Barbara E. Dodd and Patrick J. Lincoln, *Blood Group Topics* (London: Edward Arnold (Publishers) Ltd., 1975), pp. 75–84.
4. Arthur C. Guyton, *Textbook of Medical Physiology,* (Philadelphia: W. B. Saunders Company, 2nd edn., May, 1983), p. 205.
5. *Ibid.*, p. 195.
6. Titmuss, *The Gift Relationship,* pp. 28–9.
7. *Family Health Guide and Medical Encyclopaedia* (New York: Reader's Digest Association, 1980), pp. 331–2, 357, 450 and 564.
8. Titmuss, *The Gift Relationship*, p. 29.

Chapter 7

1. Muftī Muḥammad Shafīʿ, *Insānī Aʿḍā' kī Paiwandkārī – Sharīʿat Islāmiyyah kī Roshnī main,* (Karachi: Dār al-Ishāʿat, 1967), p. 24.
2. For the original Arabic text see Muḥammad Idrīs al-Shāfiʿī, *Kitāb al-Umm* (Beirut: Dār al-Maʿrifah li al-Ṭibāʿah wa al-Nashr, n.d.), vol. 1, p. 54.
3. Shafīʿ, *Insānī Aʿḍā'*, p. 24.
4. *Ibid.*
5. *Ibid.*
6. *Ibid.*
7. *Ibid.*, pp. 25–6.

8. Aḥmad Fahmī Abū Sinnah, 'Ḥukm al-ʿIlāj bi Naql Dam al-Insān aw Naql Aʿḍā' aw Ajzā' minhā' in *Majallat al-Majmaʿ al-Fiqhī* (1408 AH/ 1987), pp. 23–4.
9. *Ibid.*, p. 24.
10. See Ẓāhir, *Ḥiwār Maʿ Ṭābīb Muslim*, p. 83.
11. Abū Sinnah, 'Ḥukm al-ʿIlāj', p. 24.
12. ʿAbd al-Salām al-Shukrī, *Naql wa Zirāʿat al-Aʿḍā' al-Ādamiyyah min Manẓūr al-Islāmī*, (Nicosia: Al-Dār al-Maṣriyyah li al-Nashr wa al-Tawzīʿ, 1409 AH/1989), pp. 182–4.
13. *Ibid.*, p. 184.
14. *Ibid.*
15. Jād al-Ḥaqq, *Buḥūth wa Fatāwā al-Islāmīyah*, vol. 3, p. 451.
16. Mannāʿ ibn Khalīl al-Qaṭṭān, 'Al-Ijtihād al-Fiqhī li al-Tabarruʿ bi al-Dam wa Naqlih' in *Majallat al-Majmaʿ al-Fiqhī* (1410 AH/ 1989), p. 47.
17. Ḥasanayn Muḥammad Makhlūf, *Fatāwā Sharīʿah,* (Cairo: Maṭbaʿat al-Madanī, 1971), vol. 2, p. 218.
18. Titmuss, *The Gift Relationship,* p. 71.
19. *Ibid.*, pp. 75–89.
20. Abū Sinnah, 'Ḥukm al-ʿIlāj', p. 24.
21. 'Qarārāt al-Majmaʿ al-Fiqhī' in *Majjalat al-Majmaʿ al-Fiqhī* (1408–1410 AH), p. 83.
22. Al-Shukrī, *Naql wa Zirāʿat,* p. 180.
23. Abū Sinnah, 'Ḥukm al-ʿIlāj', p. 24. The average person has 8 to 9 pints of blood in his body; normally only one pint of blood is taken at one sitting as more might harm the donor.
24. *Ṣaḥīḥ al-Bukhārī,* 'Kitāb al-Buyūʿ', vol. 3, p. 111.
25. Jād al-Ḥaqq, *Buḥūth wa Fatāwā al-Islāmīyah*, vol. 3, pp. 442–3.
26. Shafīʿ, *Insānī Aʿḍā'*, p. 26.
27. *Ibid.*, pp. 27–8, for the Arabic text.
28. *Qarārāt al-Majmaʿ al-Fiqhī* (1408–1410 AH), p. 83.
29. Titmuss, *The Gift Relationship,* pp. 28–9.
30. Abū Sinnah, 'Ḥukm al-ʿIlāj', p. 24.
31. The author of this work may be Abū al-ʿAbbās Aḥmad ʿUmar al-Qurṭubī who was an eminent Mālikī jurist (*faqīh)* born in Cordova in 578 AH/ 1173, and died in Alexandria in 656 AH/1259.
32. For a similar statement refer to Abū ʿAbd Allāh ibn Aḥmad ibn Muḥammad ibn Qudāmah, *Al-Mughnī* (Cairo: Maktabah al-Jamhūriyyah al-ʿArabiyyah, n.d.), vol. 8, p. 597.
33. Jād al-Ḥaqq, *Buḥūth wa Fatāwā al-Islāmīyah*, vol. 3, p. 452.
34. Shafīʿ, *Insānī Aʿḍā'*, p. 28.
35. See ʿAbd Allāh ʿAbd al-Raḥmān al-Bassām, 'Zirāʿat al-Aʿḍā' al-Insāniyyah fī Jism al-Insān', in *Majallat al-Majmaʿ al-Fiqhī* (1408 AH/ 1987), p. 22.

Chapter 8

1. See al-Shukrī, *Naql wa Zirāʿat,* p. 125.
2. Muḥammad Amīn ibn ʿUmar ibn ʿĀbidīn, *Hāshiyah Radd al-Muḥtār,* (Beirut: Dār al-Fikr al-ʿArabī, n.d.), vol. 5, p. 58.
3. See al-Shukrī, *Naql wa Zirāʿat,* p. 127.
4. Muḥammad ibn Aḥmad ibn Jazī al-Gharnāṭī al-Mālikī, *Qawānīn al-Aḥkām al-Sharʿīyah wa Masā'il al-Furūʿ al-Fiqhiyyah* (Beirut: Dār al-ʿIlm li al-Malāyīn, 1979), p. 194.
5. See al-Shukrī, *Naql wa Zirāʿat,* p. 129.
6. A *Kāfir* means an unbeliever and a *dhimmī* is a person of the *Ahl al-Kitāb* (i.e. a Jew or Christian) residing in an Islamic state.
7. See al-Shukrī, *Naql wa Zirāʿat,* p. 130.
8. For the relevant Arabic text see al-Shukrī, *Naql wa Zirāʿat,* p. 132.

Chapter 9

1. See Shafīʿ, *Insānī Aʿḍā'*, pp. 29–38.
2. *Sermons of the Holy Prophet Muḥammad,* (Islamabad: Daʿwah-o-Irshād Wing of the Islamic Research Institute, Shaʿbān 1400 AH), p. 31.
3. ʿAbd al-Qādir ʿAwdah, *Al-Tashrīʿ al-Jinā'ī al-Islāmī Muqāranah bi al-Qānūn al-Waḍaʿī* (Cairo: Dār al-Turāth al-ʿArabī, n.d.), vol. 2, p. 5.
4. Abū Dāwūd, *Sunan Abī Dāwūd,* 'Kitāb al-Janā'iz', ḥadīth no. 3207, vol. 2, pp. 212–13.
5. Shafīʿ, *Insānī Aʿḍā'*, p. 37.
6. Abū Dāwūd, *Sunan Abī Dāwūd,* 'Kitāb al-Tarajjul', ḥadīth no. 4168, vol. 2, p. 77.
7. Charles Hamilton, *The Hedaya,* (Lahore: The Premier Book House, 1963), p. 270.
8. Al-Shukrī, *Naql wa Zirāʿat,* p. 134.
9. Abū Dāwūd, *Sunan Abī Dāwūd,* 'Kitāb al-Janā'iz', ḥadīth no. 3207, vol. 2, pp. 212–13.
10. See al-Shukrī, *Naql wa Zirāʿat,* p. 125.
11. Abū Dāwūd, *Sunan Abī Dāwūd,* 'Kitāb al-Janā'iz', ḥadīth no. 3207, vol. 2, pp. 212–13.
12. See al-Shukrī, *Naql wa Zirāʿat,* pp. 136–7.
13. *Ṣaḥīḥ al-Bukhārī,* 'Kitāb al-Dhabā'iḥ wa al-Ṣayd', vol. 3, pp. 121–2.
14. Al-Shukrī, *Naql wa Zirāʿat,* p. 137.
15. For example see the arguments put forward in favour of organ transplantation by Shaykh ʿAbd al-Raḥmān al-Bassām and Shaykh Muḥammad Rashīd Riḍā Qabbānī, 'Zirāʿat al-Aʿḍā' al-Insāniyyah fī Jism al-Insān' in *Majallat al-Majmaʿ al-Fiqhī* (1408 AH/1987), pp. 13–22 and 27–33.
16. Abū Zahrah, *Uṣūl al-Fiqh,* pp. 299 and 301.
17. Ibn Qudāmah, *al-Mughnī,* vol. 2, p. 551.

18. S.M. Darsh, *Islamic Health Rules,* (London: Taha Publishers, 1981), p. 3.
19. For example see Ẓāhir, *Ḥiwār Maʿ Ṭābīb Muslim*, p. 83.
20. *Ṣaḥīḥ al-Bukhārī,* 'Kitāb al-Adab', vol. 3, p. 12.
21. Ẓāhir, *Ḥiwār Maʿ Ṭābīb Muslim*, p. 85.
22. Jād al-Ḥaqq, *Buḥūth wa Fatāwā al-Islāmīyah*, vol. 3, p. 428.
23. *Ibid.*, p. 429.
24. *Fatwā* issued to Islamic Medical Association of South Africa by Dār al-Iftā', Riyadh, Saudi Arabia, p. 14.
25. See *al-Muslimūn*, a Saudi Arabian newspaper, 9–15 Rabīʿ II 1406 AH/ 21–28 December 1985, p. 85.
26. Abū ʿAbd Allāh Muḥammad ibn Yazīd ibn Mājah, *Sunan Ibn Mājah,* (Beirut: Dār al-Iḥyā' al-Kutub al-ʿArabiyyah, n.d.) 'Kitāb al-Ruhūn', ḥadīth no. 4, vol. 2, p. 816.
27. Shafīʿ, *Insānī Aʿḍā'*, p. 22.
28. Ẓāhir, *Ḥiwār Maʿ Ṭābīb Muslim*, p. 87.
29. *Fatwā* issued to Islamic Medical Association of South Africa by Dār al-Iftā', Riyadh, Saudi Arabia, p. 15.

Chapter 10

1. Islamic Fiqh Academy of India – 'Developing A Religious Law in Modern Times' in *Religion and Law Review*, p. 175.
2. *Ibid.*, p. 177.
3. *Ibid.*, p. 170.
4. 'Qarār al-Majmaʿ al-Fiqhī' in *Majallat al-Majmaʿ al-Fiqhī* (1408 AH/ 1987), p. 40.
5. 'Resolutions and Recommendations of the Fourth Session of the Council of the Islamic Fiqh Academy' in *Organisation of the Islamic Conference's Islamic Fiqh Academy – Resolutions and Recommendations,* (Jeddah: Maṭābiʿ Sharikat Dār al-ʿIlm li al-Ṭibāʿah wa al-Nashr, 1406–1409 AH/ 1985–1989), p. 52.
6. Islamic Fiqh Academy of India – 'Developing A Religious Law in Modern Times', *Review*, p. 178.
7. 'Qarār al-Majmaʿ al-Fiqhī' in *Majallat al-Majmaʿ al-Fiqhī* (1408 AH/ 1987), p. 40.
8. Islamic Fiqh Academy of India – 'Developing A Religious Law in Modern Times', p. 178.
9. 'Resolutions and Recommendations of the Fourth Session of the Council of the Islamic Fiqh Academy' (1408 AH/1988), p. 52.
10. 'Qarār al-Majmaʿ al-Fiqhī' in *Majallat al-Majmaʿ al-Fiqhī* (1408 AH/ 1987), p. 40.
11. Islamic Fiqh Academy of India – 'Developing A Religious Law in Modern Times', p. 178.

Chapter 11

1. *Ṣaḥīḥ al-Bukhārī,* 'Kitāb al-Waṣāyā', vol. 4, p. 2.
2. M.S. Omar, *An Introduction to the Islamic Law of Succession,* (Durban: Impress, 1982), p. 2.
3. ʿAlī ʿAbd al-Raḥmān al-Rabīʿah, '*Al-Waṣiyyah*' in *Majallat Majmaʿ al-Fiqhī* (1409 AH/1989), p. 69.
4. Islamic Fiqh Academy of India – 'Developing A Religious Law in Modern Times', p. 179.
5. Tanzīlur Raḥmān, *A Code of Muslim Personal Law*, (Karachi: Islamic Publishers, 1980), vol. 2, p. 330.
6. See 'Qarār al-Majmaʿ al-Fiqhī' in *Majallat al-Majmaʿ al-Fiqhī* (1408 AH/1987), p. 40.
7. 'Resolutions and Recommendations of the Fourth Session of the Council of the Islamic Fiqh Academy' (1408 AH/1988), pp. 52–3.
8. *A Code of Muslim Personal Law*, *op. cit.*, vol. 2, p. 341.
9. Islamic Fiqh Academy of India – 'Developing A Religious Law in Modern Times', p. 179.
10. Tanzīlur-Raḥmān, *A Code of Muslim Personal Law,* vol. 2, p. 327.
11. From a document issued by Muslim Judicial Council, Cape Town, South Africa which was signed by Sheikh Nazim Mohammed (as President) and Maulānā Yūsuf Karaan (as Head – Fatwā Committee).

Chapter 12

1. Ibrahim B. Syed, 'Human Cloning' in *Hamdard Islamicus*, (Karachi: Bait al-Hikmah, 1999), 40 (3), 1998, p. 111.
2. *ibid.*, p. 115.
3. For an explanation of the laws of inheritance see T.P. Hughes, *Dictionary of Islam*, (Lahore: Premier Book House, n.d.), pp. 297–310.
4. *Ṣaḥīḥ Muslim*, 'Kitāb al-Salām', ḥadīth no. 68, vol. 5, p. 51.
5. According to the *fatwā* (religious decree) issued to the Islamic Medical Association of South Africa by Dār al-Iftā', Riyadh, Saudi Arabia, it is not permissible to abort defective foetuses. Fatwā no. 2484, dated 16–07–1403 AH.
6. For the legal consequences for foeticide see Abul Fadl Mohsin Ebrahim, *Abortion, Birth Control and Surrogate Parenting: An Islamic Perspective*, (Indianapolis: American Trust Publications, 1991), pp. 97–102.
7. To enter into matrimony implies the fulfilment of the *Sunnah* (practice) of the Prophet Muḥammad ﷺ which is deemed highly desirable.
8. Sacrificing the lives of the human clones for our own benefit would be tantamount to murder. See Qur'ān, 5:32.
9. For example, the thief's hand is severed as a form of punishment. See Qur'ān, 5:41.
10. *Sunan Abī Dāwūd*, 'Kitāb al-Ṭibb', part 4, p. 3.

11. See *al-Muslimūn*, a Saudi Arabian newspaper, 9–15 Rabīʿ II, 1406 AH/ 21–28 December 1985, p. 85.
12. *Sunan Ibn Mājah*, 'Kitāb al-Ruhūn', ḥadīth no. 4, vol. 2, p. 816.
13. See *Jarīdat al-ʿĀlam al-Islāmī*, (Makkah: al-ʿĀlam al-Islāmī, 3–9 Rabīʿ I, 1418 AH/7–13 July 1997), p. 4.

Chapter 13

1. Al-Sherbini, 'Iṣām, Life and Death between Physicians and Fiqh Scholars' in I.O.M.S., *Human Life: Its Inception and End as Viewed by Islam*, (Kuwait: Islamic Organization for Medical Sciences (I.O.M.S.), 1989, p. 325; and al-Mahdī, Mukhtār, 'The End of Human Life' in *ibid.*, p. 316.
2. Ebrahim, A.F.M. and Haffejee, A.A., *The Sharīʿah and Organ Transplants*, (Durban: Islamic Medical Association of South Africa. 1989), p. 7.
3. Bernard Haring, *Medical Ethics,* (Slough: England, St Paul Publications, 1972), p. 131.
4. Catherine Lyons, *Organ Transplants: The Moral Issues*, (London: SMC Press Ltd., 1970), p. 50.
5. *Ibid.*, p. 50.
6. *Ibid.*, p. 51.
7. *Ibid.*, p. 52.
8. *Ibid.*, p. 56.
9. Al-Qāḍī, Aḥmad, 'The Heart and its Relation to Life: Introduction to the Discussion of When Life Ends' in I.O.M.S., p. 361.
10. Harmon L. Smith, *Ethics and the New Medicine*, (Tennessee: Abingdon Press, 1970), p. 130.
11. Haring, *Medical Ethics*, p. 132.
12. Al-Mahdī, 'The End of Human Life' in *Human Life: Its Inception and End as Viewed by Islam*' in I.O.M.S., p. 315.
13. Ebrahim and Haffejee, *The Sharīʿah and Organ Transplants*, p. 9.
14. Martyn Evans, 'Dying to Help: Moral Questions in Organ Procurement' in Dickenson and Johnson (eds.) *Death, Dying and Bereavement*, (London: Sage Publications Ltd., 1993), p. 136.
15. Ebrahim and Haffejee, *The Sharīʿah and Organ Transplants*, p. 9.

Chapter 14

1. ʿImād al-Dīn Abū al-Fidā' ibn Kathīr, *Tafsīr al-Qur'ān al-ʿAẓīm*, (Beirut: Dār Iḥyā' al-Turāth al-ʿArabī, 1388 AH/1969), vol. 4, pp. 150–1.
2. Muḥammad al-Ḥusayn al-Dāmaghānī, *Qāmūs al-Qur'ān aw Iṣlāḥ al-Wujūh wa al-Naẓā'ir fī al-Qur'ān al-Karīm*, (Beirut: Dār al-ʿIlm li al-Malāyīn, 4th edition, 1983), pp. 492–3.
3. *Ibid.*, p. 212.
4. *Ṣaḥīḥ Muslim*, 'Kitāb al-Janā'iz', ḥadīth no. 7, vol.2, p. 634.

5. Edward William Lane, *Arabic-English Lexicon* (New York: Frederick Ungar Publishing Co., 1955), Bk. 1, pt. 1, p. 25.
6. Sayyid Quṭb, *Fī Ẓilāl al-Qur'ān*, (Beirut: Dār al-Shurūq, 1396 AH/1976), vol. 4, p. 2249.

Chapter 15

1. Tawfīq al-Wā'il, 'The Truth about Death and Life in the Qur'ān and the Stipulations of Islamic Law' in I.O.M.S., p. 452.
2. The Arabic term *ʿiddah* means the waiting period that a widow or divorcee has to observe before she may remarry. For the widow, the *ʿiddah* begins immediately upon the demise of the husband; for one who is pregnant, it ends upon giving birth. Under normal conditions, the *ʿiddah* ends four months and ten days after the death of the husband.
3. Al-Wā'il, 'The Truth about Death and Life in the Qur'ān and the Stipulations of Islamic Law' in I.O.M.S., p. 453.
4. Ibn Qudāmah, *Al-Mughnī,* vol. 2, p. 452.
5. Abū Ḥāmid ibn Muḥammad al-Ghazālī, *Iḥyā' ʿUlūm al-Dīn*, (Cairo: Maṭbaʿat al-Istiqāmah, n.d.), vol. 4, pp. 493–4.
6. Mujāhid al-Islām Qāsimī, 'Dimāghī Mawt wa Ḥayāt kā Naẓriyah aur us par Paydā Hone Wāle Fiqhī Sawālāt' in *Bahth-o-Naẓar* (Delhi: Bharat Offset Press, Ramaḍān, Ṣafar, Dhū al-Qaʿdah 1409 AH/ April, May, June 1988), vol. 5, p. 13.
7. Al-Wā'il, 'The Truth about Death and Life in the Qur'ān and the Stipulations of Islamic Law' in I.O.M.S., p. 434.
8. Al-Ghazālī, *Iḥyā' ʿUlūm al-Dīn*, vol. 3, p. 3.
9. Muḥammad Naʿīm Yāsīn, 'The End of Human Life in the Light of the Opinions of Muslim Scholars and Medical Findings' in I.O.M.S., p. 380.
10. Al-Wā'il, 'The Truth about Death and Life in the Qur'ān and the Stipulations of Islamic Law' in I.O.M.S., p. 435.
11. Qāsimī, 'Dimāghī Mawt', pp. 13–14.
12. Yāsīn, 'The End of Human Life in the Light of the Opinions of Muslim Scholars and Medical Findings' in I.O.M.S., p. 388.
13. *Ibid.*, p. 389.
14. Al-Ghazālī, *Iḥyā' ʿUlūm al-Dīn*, vol. 4 , p. 494.
15. Aḥmad Shawqī Ibrāhīm, 'The End of Human Life' in I.O.M.S., p. 348 and al-Qāḍī, 'The Heart and its Relation to Life' in I.O.M.S., p. 363.
16. Khaled al-Mazkur, *et. el.* (eds.), 'Report on the Fifth Session' in I.O.M.S., p. 516.
17. Qāsimī, 'Dimāghī Mawt', p. 14.
18. Yāsīn, 'The End of Human Life in the Light of the Opinions of Muslim Scholars' in I.O.M.S., pp. 389–90.
19. Muṣṭafā Ṣabrī Ardughdu, 'The End of Human Life' in I.O.M.S., p. 468.
20. Al-Wā'il, 'The Truth about Death and Life in the Qur'ān and the Stipulations of Islamic Law' in I.O.M.S., p. 445.
21. Muḥammad Sulaymān al-Ashqar, 'The End of Life' in I.O.M.S., pp. 402–3.

22. Badr al-Mutawallī ʿAbd al-Bāsiṭ, 'The End of Human Life as Viewed, by Islam' in I.O.M.S., p. 417 and ʿAbd al-Qādir ibn Muḥammad al-ʿAmarī, 'The End of Life' in I.O.M.S., p. 458.
23. Muḥammad al-Mukhtār al-Salāmī, 'When Does Life End?' in I.O.M.S., pp. 422–3.
24. Al-Wā'il, 'The Truth about Death and Life in the Qur'ān and the Stipulations of Islamic Law' in I.O.M.S., p. 445.

Chapter 16

1. From the recommendations of the Seminar as published in I.O.M.S., p. 629.
2. Resolution No. 5 of the Third Session of the Council of the Islamic Fiqh Academy (1407 AH/1986) in *Organisation of the Islamic Conference's Islamic Fiqh Academy: Resolutions and Recommendations*, (Jeddah: Maṭābiʿ Sharikat Dār al-ʿIlm li al-Ṭibāʿah wa al-Nashr, 1406–1409 AH/1985–1989), p. 30.
3. See al-Qarār al-Thānī bi Sha'n Taqrīr Ḥuṣūl al-Wafāt wa Rafʿ Ajhijah al-Inʿāsh min Jism al-Insān' in *Majallat Majmaʿ al-Fiqhī,* (1412 AH), p. 21.
4. Qāsimī, 'Dimāghī Mawt', p. 15.
5. Jād al-Ḥaqq, *Qaḍāyā Islāmiyyah Muʿāṣarah: Al-Fiqh al-Islāmī Murūnatuh wa Taṭawwuruh,* (Cairo: Maṭbaʿah al-Azhariyyah, 1410 AH/1989), p. 249.
6. From a document of Majlis al-Shurā al-Islāmī dated 10 July, 1993, addressed to the Medical Superintendent, Groote Schuur Hospital, Observatory, Cape Town, South Africa, p. 4.
7. A.K. Toffar, 'Organ Transplantations – A Sharīʿah Perspective', unpublished article, dated Muḥarram 1415 AH/June 1994, p. 6.
8. Qāsimī, 'Dimāghī Mawt', p. 15.
9. From a document issued by the Muslim Judicial Council, Cape Town, South Africa which was signed by Sheikh Nazim Mohammed (as President) and Mawlānā Yūsuf Karaan (as Head: Fatwā Committee).
10. Resolution No. 1 of the Fourth Session of the Council of the Islamic Fiqh Academy (1408 AH/1988) in *Organisation of the Islamic Conference's Islamic Fiqh Academy: Resolutions and Recommendations*, (1406–1409 AH/1985–1989), p. 52.
11. Here it may mean that that person is brain stem dead and on life support apparatus.
12. Ardughdu, 'The End of Human Life' in I.O.M.S., p. 468.
13. Al-Salāmī, 'When Does Life End?' in I.O.M.S., p. 428.
14. See 'al-Qarār al-Thānī' in *Majallat Majmaʿ al-Fiqhī*, (1412 AH), p. 21.
15. From a document issued by the Muslim Judicial Council, Cape Town, South Africa which was signed by Sheikh Nazim Mohammed (as President) and Mawlānā Yūsuf Karaan (as Head: Fatwā Committee)

16. From a document issued by Majlis al-ʿUlamā' of South Africa, Port Elizabeth, South Africa, addressed to Dr S.A. Wadee dated 2nd Ramaḍān 1414 AH/14th February 1994, p. 2.

Chapter 17

1. *Stedman's Illustrated Medical Dictionary*, (Baltimore: Williams & Wilkins, 24th edn., 1982), p. 494.
2. Muḥammad Quṭb, *Islam the Misunderstood Religion*, (Stuttgart: Ernst Klett Publishers, 1971), p. 135.
3. Al-Jazīrī, *Kitāb al-Fiqh ʿalā Madhāhib al-Arbaʿah*, vol. 5, p. 226.
4. Muḥammad Asad, *The Message of the Qur'ān*, p. 423, n. 38.
5. Mawlānā Fazlul Karim, *Al-Hadis*, (Lahore: The Book House, 1939), vol. 2, p. 514.
6. Karim, *Al Hadis*, vol. 1, p. 319.
7. Resolution No. 5 of the Third Session of the Council of the Islamic Fiqh Academy (1407 AH/1986) in *Organisation of the Islamic Conference's Islamic Fiqh Academy: Resolutions and Recommendations* (1406–1409 AH/1985–1989), p. 30.
8. Fazlur Rahman, *Health and Medicine in the Islamic Tradition*, (New York: The Crossroad Publishing Company, 1989), pp. 69–70.
9. Christiaan Barnard, *Good Life Good Death – A Doctor's Case for Euthanasia and Suicide*, (Cape Town: Howard Timmins (Pty) Ltd., 1980), p. 114.
10. *Ṣaḥīḥ al-Bukhārī*, 'Kitāb al-Ṭibb', vol. 3, p. 153.
11. *Ibid.*, p. 156.

Conclusion

1. Anees (ed.), *Health Sciences in Early Islam*, vol. 2, p. 364.
2. *Ṣaḥīḥ Muslim*, 'Kitāb al-Salām', ḥadīth no. 68. vol. 5, p. 51.
3. For a detailed account of the functions of blood see A.W. Sloan, *Physiology for Students and Teachers of Physical Education*, (London: Edward Arnold (Publishers) Ltd., 1970), pp. 43–4.
4. David Lamb, 'Organ Transplants' in Dickenson and Johnson, p. 131.
5. Al-Ashqar, 'The End of Life' in I.O.M.S., p. 408.
6. Al-Wā'il, 'The Truth about Death and Life in the Qur'ān and the Stipulations of Islamic Law' in I.O.M.S., pp. 449–50.
7. Muḥammad ʿAbdullāh, 'The End of Human Life' in I.O.M.S., p. 370.
8. *Ibid.*
9. Resolution No. 1 of the Fourth Session of the Council of the Islamic Fiqh Academy (1408 AH/1988) in *Organisation of the Islamic Conference's Islamic Fiqh Academy – Resolutions and Recommendations* (1406–1409 AH/1985–1989), p. 52.
10. From the recommendations of the Seminar as published in I.O.M.S., p. 629.

BIBLIOGRAPHY

A. Arabic Sources

BOOKS

Abū Dāwūd, Sulaymān ibn al-Ashʿath al-Sijistānī, *Sunan Abī Dāwūd*. Beirut: Dār Iḥyā' al-Sunnah al-Nabawiyyah, n.d., 2 vols.

Abū Zahrah, Muḥammad, *Uṣūl al-Fiqh*. Cairo: Dār al-Fikr al-ʿArabī, n.d.

ʿAwdah, ʿAbd al-Qādir, *Al-Tashrīʿ al-Jinā'ī al-Islāmī Muqāranah bi al-Qānūn al-Waḍaʿī*. Cairo: Dār al-Turāth al-ʿArabī, n.d., 2 vols.

Al-Bukhārī, Muḥammad ibn Ismāʿīl, *Ṣaḥīḥ al-Bukhārī*. Cairo: Dār al-Shaʿb, n.d., 3 vols.

Al-Dāmaghānī, Muḥammad al-Ḥusayn, *Qāmūs al-Qur'ān aw Iṣlāḥ al-Wujūh wa al-Naẓā'ir fī al-Qur'ān al-Karīm*. Beirut: Dār al-ʿIlm li al-Malāyīn, 4th edn., 1983.

Al-Ghazālī, Abū Ḥāmid ibn Muḥammad, *Iḥyā' ʿUlūm al-Dīn*. Cairo: Maṭbaʿat al-Istiqāmah, n.d., 4 vols.

Ibn ʿĀbidīn, Muḥammad Amīn ibn ʿUmar, *Hāshiyah Radd al-Muḥtār*. Beirut: Dār al Fikr al-ʿArabī, n.d., 8 vols.

Ibn Jazī al-Gharnāṭī al-Mālikī, Muḥammad ibn Aḥmad *Qawānīn Aḥkām al-Sharʿīyah wa Masā'il al-Furūʿ al-Fiqhiyyah*. Beirut: Dār al-ʿIlm li al-Malāyīn, 1979.

Ibn Kathīr, ʿImād al-Dīn Abū al-Fidā', *Tafsīr al-Qur'ān al-ʿAẓīm*. Beirut: Dār Iḥyā' al-Turāth al-ʿArabī, 1388 AH/1969, 4 vols.

Ibn Mājah, Abū ʿAbd Allāh Muḥammad ibn Yazīd, *Sunan Ibn Mājah*. Beirut: Dār al-Iḥyā' al-Kutub al-ʿArabiyyah, n.d., 2 vols.

Ibn Qudāmah, Muḥammad ʿAbd Allāh Aḥmad Muḥammad, *Al-Mughnī*. Cairo: Maktabat al-Jamhūriyyah al-ʿArabiyyah, n.d., 9 vols.

Ibn Rushd, Abū al-Walīd Muḥammad Aḥmad (al-Qurṭubī), *Bidāyat al-Mujtahid wa Nihāyat al-Muqtaṣid,* Cairo: Maṭbaʿah Muṣṭafā al-Bābī al-Ḥalabī wa Awlāduh, 1981, 2 vols.

Jād al-Ḥaqq, ʿAlī Jād al-Ḥaqq, *Qaḍāyā Islāmiyyah Muʿāṣarah: Al-Fiqh al-Islāmī Murūnatuh wa Taṭawwuruh*. Cairo: Maṭbaʿah al-Azhariyyah, 1410 AH/1989, – *Buḥūth wa Fatāwā Islāmiyyah Fī Qaḍāyā Muʿāṣarah*. Cairo: Al-Azhar University, 1994, 4 vols.

al-Jazīrī, ʿAbd al-Raḥmān, *Kitāb al-Fiqh ʿalā al-Madhāhib al-Arbaʿah*. Beirut: Dār al-Fikr al-ʿArabī, n.d., 5 vols.

Makhlūf, Ḥasanayn Muḥammad, *Fatāwā Sharʿīyah*. Cairo: Maṭbaʿat al-Madanī, 1971, 2 vols.

Al-Nasā'ī, Abū ʿAbd al-Raḥmān Aḥmad ibn Shuʿayb, *Sunan al-Nasā'ī*. Cairo: Al-Maktabah al-Tājārīyah, 1398 AH/1978, 4 vols.

Al-Nawawī, Muḥy al-Dīn Abū Zakarīyā Yaḥyā ibn Sharaf, *Riyāḍ al-Ṣāliḥīn*. Lahore: Idārat al-Sunnah, 1398 AH/1978.

Al-Naysābūrī, Muslim ibn al-Ḥajjāj, *Ṣaḥīḥ Muslim*. Cairo: Dār al-Shaʿb, n.d., 5 vols.

Al-Qaraḍāwī, Yūsuf, *Al-Ḥalāl wa al-Ḥarām fī al-Islām*. Cairo: Maktabah Wahbah, 1400 AH/1980.

Quṭb, Sayyid, *Fī Ẓilāl al-Qur'ān*. Beirut: Dār al-Shurūq, 1396 AH/1976, 6 vols.

Al-Shāfiʿī, Muḥammad ibn Idrīs, *Kitāb al-Umm*. Beirut: Dār al-Maʿrifah li al-Ṭibāʿah wa al-Nashr, n.d., 4 vols.

Al-Shukrī, ʿAbd al-Salām, *Naql wa Zirāʿat al-Aʿḍā' al-Ādamiyyah min Manẓūr al-Islāmī*, (Nicosia: Al-Dār al-Maṣrīyah li al-Nashr wa al-Tawzīʿ, 1409 AH/ 1989.

Al-Tirmidhī, Abū ʿĪsā Muḥammad ibn ʿĪsā, *Sunan al-Tirmidhī*. Al-Madīnah al-Munawwarah: Al-Maktabah al-Salafiyyah,1394 AH/1974, 5 vols.

Ẓāhir, Fayṣal Ibrāhīm, *Ḥiwār Maʿ Ṭābīb Muslim*. Cairo: Al-Risālah, n.d.

ARTICLES

Abū Sinnah, Aḥmad Fahmī, 'Ḥukm al-ʿIlāj bi Naql Dam al-Insān aw Naql Aʿḍā' aw Ajzā' minhā' in *Majallat al-Majmaʿ al-Fiqhī*. Makkah: Rābiṭat al-ʿĀlam al-Islāmī, 1408 AH/1987.

Al-Bassām, ʿAbd Allāh ʿAbd al-Raḥmān, 'Zirāʿat al-Aʿḍā' al-Insāniyyah fi Jism al-Insān' in *Majallat al-Majmaʿ al-Fiqhī*. Makkah: Rābiṭat al-ʿĀlam al-Islāmī, 1408 AH/1987.

Fatwā issued to Islamic Medical Association of South Africa by Dār al-Iftā'. Riyadh, n.d.

Jarīdat al-ʿĀlam al-Islāmī. Makkah: Rābiṭat al-ʿĀlam al-Islāmī, 3–9 *Rabīʿ* I, 1418 AH/7–13 July 1997.

Qabbānī, ʿAbd al-Raḥmān al-Rashīd Riḍā, 'Zirāʿat al-Aʿḍā' al-Insāniyyah fī Jism al-Insān' in *Majallat al-Majmaʿ al-Fiqhī,* 1408 AH/1987.

'Al-Qarār al-Awwal bi Sha'n Mawḍūʿ Zirāʿat al-Aʿḍā'' in *Qarārāt Majlis al-Majmaʿ al-Fiqhī al-Islāmī*. Makkah: Rābiṭat al-ʿĀlam al-Islāmī, 1405 AH/ 1985.

'Qarār al-Majmaʿ al-Fiqhī bi Sha'n Mawḍūʿ Zirāʿat al-Aʿḍā'' in *Majallat al-Majmaʿ al-Fiqhī*. Makkah: Rābiṭat al-ʿĀlam al-Islāmī, 1408 AH/1987.

'Qarārāt al-Majmaʿ al-Fiqhī' in *Majallat al-Majmaʿ al-Fiqhī*, 1408–1410 AH.

'Al-Qarār al-Thānī bi Sha'n Taqrīr Ḥuṣūl al-Wafāt wa Rafʿ Ajhijah al-Inʿāsh min Jism al-Insān' in *Majallat Majmaʿ al-Fiqhī,* 1412 AH.

Al-Qaṭṭān, Mannāʿ ibn Khalīl, 'Al-Ijtihād al-Fiqhī li al-Tabarruʿ bi al-Dam wa Naqlih' in *Majallat al-Majmaʿ al-Fiqhī*, 1410 AH/ 1989.

Al-Rabīʿah, ʿAlī ʿAbd al-Raḥmān '*Al-Waṣiyyah*' in *Majallat Majmaʿ al-Fiqhī*, 1409 AH/1989.

B. Urdu Sources

BOOKLET

Muftī Muḥammad Shafīʿ, *Insānī Aʿḍā' kī Paiwandkārī – Sharīʿat Islāmiyyah kī Roshnī main*. Karachi: Dār al-Ishāʿat, 1967.

ARTICLE

Mujāhid al-Islām Qāsimī, 'Dimāghī Mawt wa Ḥayāt kā Naẓrīyah aur us par Paydā Hone Wāle Fiqhī Sawālāt' in *Baḥth-o-Naẓar*. Delhi: Bharat Offset Press, Ramaḍān, Ṣafar, Dhū al-Qaʿdah 1409 AH.

C. English Sources

BOOKS

Anees, Munawar A. (ed.), *Health Sciences in Early Islam*. Texas: Noor Health Foundation/Zahra Publications, 1983. 2 vols.
Ansari, Muḥammad Fazlur Raḥmān, *The Qur'ānic Foundations and Structure of Muslim Society*. Karachi: Trade and Industry Publications Ltd., 1973. 2 vols.
Asad, Muḥammad, *The Message of the Qur'ān*. Gibraltar: Dar al-Andalus Limited, 1980.
Barnard, Christiaan, *Good Life Good Death – A Doctor's Case for Euthanasia and Suicide*. Cape Town: Howard Timmins (Pty) Ltd., 1980.
Brown, Colin (ed.), *The New International Dictionary of New Testament Theology*. Exeter: The Paternoster Press Ltd., 1975. 3 vols.
Chambers's Encyclopaedia. London: George Newnes Ltd., 1959. 15 vols.
Darsh, S.M., *Islamic Health Rules*. London: Taha Publishers, 1981.
Dodd, Barbara E. and Lincoln, Patrick J., *Blood Group Topics*. London: Edward Arnold (Publishers) Ltd., 1975.
Dickenson, Donna and Johnson, Malcolm (eds.), *Death, Dying and Bereavement*. London: Sage Publications Ltd., 1993.
Ebling, E.J. (ed.), *Biology and Ethics*. Proceedings of a Symposium held at the Royal Geographical Society, London, 26–27 Sept. 1968. London: Academic Press, 1969.
Ebrahim, A.F.M. and Haffejee, A.A., *The Sharīʿah and Organ Transplants*. Durban: Islamic Medical Association of South Africa, 1989.
Ebrahim, Abul Fadl Mohsin, *Abortion, Birth Control and Surrogate Parenting: An Islamic Perspective*. Indianapolis: American Trust Publications, 1991.
Encyclopaedia Britannica, London: Encyclopaedia Britannica Inc., 1971. 26 vols.
Family Health Guide and Medical Encyclopaedia. New York: Reader's Digest Association Inc., 1980.
Guyton, Arthur C., *Textbook of Medical Physiology*. Philadelphia: W. B. Saunders Company, 2nd. edn., 1983.

Hamilton, Charles, *The Hedaya,* Lahore: The Premier Book House, 1963.
Haring, Bernard, *Medical Ethics*, Slough: St. Paul Publications, 1972.
Hathout, Hassan, *Topics in Islamic Medicine*. Kuwait: International Organisation of Islamic Medicine, 1st edn., 1984.
Hughes, T.P., *Dictionary of Islam.* Lahore: Premier Book House, n.d.
Stedman's Illustrated Medical Dictionary. Baltimore: Williams & Wilkins, 24th edn., 1982.
I.O.M.S., *Human Life: Its Inception and End as Viewed by Islam*. Kuwait: International Organization for Medical Sciences (I.O.M.S.), 1989.
Iqbal, Afzal, *Culture of Islam,* Lahore: Institute of Islamic Culture, 1974.
Karim, Fazlul, *Al-Hadis*. Lahore: The Book House, 1939. 4 vols.
Lane, Edward William, *Arabic-English Lexicon*. New York: Frederick Ungar Publishing Co., 1955. 8 vols.
Lyons, Catherine. *Organ Transplants: The Moral Issues*. London: SMC Press Ltd., 1970.
Masri, al-Ḥāfiẓ B.A., *Animals in Islam*. Petersfield: The Athene Trust, 1989.
Omar, M.S., *An Introduction to the Islamic Law of Succession*. Durban: Impress, 1982.
Quṭb, M., *Islam the Misunderstood Religion*. Stuttgart: Ernst Klett Publishers, 1971.
Rahman, Fazlur, *Health and Medicine in the Islamic Tradition*. New York: The Crossroad Publishing Company, 1989.
Robson, James, *Mishkāt al-Maṣābīḥ* (Eng. trans.). Lahore: Sh. Muḥammad Ashraf, 1964. 4 vols.
Sa'īd, Hakim Mohammed (ed.), *Al-Birūnī Commemorative Volume.* Proceedings of the International Congress in Commemoration of the Millenary of Abū Rayḥān Muḥammad ibn Aḥmad al-Bīrūnī, Karachi, Nov. 26 – Dec. 12, 1973. Karachi: Hamdard National Foundation, 1979.
Sermons of the Holy Prophet Muḥammad. Islamabad: Da'wah-o-Irshād Wing of the Islamic Research Institute, 1400 AH.
Sherwani, M.H.K., *Ḥaḍrat Abū Bakr, the First Caliph of Islam*. (Trans. by S.M. Ḥaq). Lahore: Sh. Muḥammad Ashraf, 1959.
Sloan, A.W., *Physiology for Students and Teachers of Physical Education*. London: Edward Arnold (Publishers) Ltd., 1970.
Titmuss, Richard M., *The Gift Relationship from Human Blood to Social Policy*. London: George Allen & Unwin Ltd., 1970.
Smith, Harmon L., *Ethics and the New Medicine*. Tennessee: Abingdon Press, 1970.
Tanzīlur Raḥmān, *A Code of Muslim Personal Law.* Karachi: Islamic Publishers, 1980. 2 vols.
The New Universal Encyclopaedia. London: The Amalgamated Press Ltd., n.d. 15 vols.
Tuffery, A.A. (ed.), *Laboratory Animals: An Introduction for New Experiments,* London: John Wiley & Sons Ltd., 1987.

ARTICLES

ʿAbd al-Bāsiṭ, Badr al-Mutawallī, 'The End of Human Life as Viewed by Islam' in I.O.M.S. (q.v.).

Al-ʿAmārī, ʿAbd al-Qādir ibn Muḥammad, 'The End of Human Life as Viewed By Islam' in I.O.M.S. (q.v.) .

Ardughdu, Muṣṭafā Ṣabrī, 'The End Of Human Life' in I.O.M.S. (q.v.).

Al-Ashqar, Muḥammad Sulaymān, 'The End of Human Life' in I.O.M.S. (q.v.).

Barnard, Christiaan N., 'Reflections On the First Heart Transplant'. *South African Medical Journal*. Pinelands: Publications Division of the Medical Association of South Africa, 1987.

A document issued by Majlis al-Shūrā al-Islāmī dated 10 July, 1993, addressed to the Medical Superintendent, Groote Schuur Hospital, Observatory, Cape Town, South Africa.

A document issued by the Muslim Judicial Council, Cape Town, South Africa which was signed by Sheikh Nazim Mohammed (as President) and Maulānā Yūsuf Karaan (as Head: Fatwā Committee).

Evans, Martyn, 'Dying to Help: Moral Questions in Organ Procurement' in Dickenson and Johnson.

Hamarneh, Sami K., 'Al-Bīrūnī the Father of Islamic Pharmacy and Marine Biology as Demonstrated in as-Saydanah' in Hakim Mohammed Saʿīd.

Ibrāhīm, Aḥmad Shawqī, 'The End of Human Life as Viewed by Islam' in I.O.M.S. (q.v.).

Religious Law Report, 'Islamic Fiqh Academy of India – Developing a Religious Law in Modern Times' in *Religion and Law Review*, 1(1) (Summer 1992).

Lamb, David. 'Organ Transplants' in Dickenson and Johnson.

Al-Mahdī, Mukhtār, 'The End of Human Life as Viewed by Islam' in I.O.M.S. (q.v.).

Majlis al-ʿUlamā'. 'Document on Organ Transplants.'

Mazkur, Khaled (ed., *et. al.*) 'Report on the Fifth Session' in I.O.M.S. (q.v.).

'Pig to Man Transplants: It's Possible – UK Surgeon' in the *Daily News* (1 August, 1988). Durban.

Al-Qāḍī, Aḥmad, 'The Heart and its Relation to Life – Introduction to the Discussion of When Life Ends' in I.O.M.S. (q.v.).

'Recommendations' in I.O.M.S. (q.v.).

Remfry, Jenny, 'Ethical Aspects of Animal Experimentation' in Tuffery, A.A.

Resolution No. 5 of the Third Session of the Council of the Islamic Fiqh Academy (1407 AH/1986) in *Organisation of the Islamic Conference's Islamic Fiqh Academy – Resolutions and Recommendations*. Jeddah: Maṭābiʿ Sharikat Dār al-ʿIlm li al- Ṭibāʿah wa al-Nashr, 1406–1409 AH/1985–1989.

Resolution No. 1 of the Fourth Session of the Council of the Islamic Fiqh Academy (1408 AH/1988) in *Organisation of the Islamic Conference's Islamic Fiqh Academy – Resolutions and Recommendations*. Jeddah: Maṭābiʿ Sharikat Dār al-ʿIlm li al-Ṭibāʿah wa al-Nashr, 1406–1409 AH/1985–1989.

Al-Salāmī, Muḥammad al-Mukhtār, 'When Does Life End?' in I.O.M.S. (q.v.).

Al-Sherbini, ʿIṣām, 'Life and Death between Physicians and Fiqh Scholars' in I.O.M.S. (q.v.).

Syed, Ibrahim B., 'Human Cloning' in *Hamdard Islamicus* (Karachi), 40 (3), 1998.

Toffar, A.K.,'Organ Transplantations – A Sharīʿah Perspective.' Unpublished article, dated Muḥarram 1415 AH/June 1994.

Al-Wā'il, Tawfīq.'The Truth about Death and Life in the Qur'ān and the Stipulations of Islamic Law' in I.O.M.S. (q.v.) 1989.

Woodruff, M.A., 'The Ethics of Organ Transplantation' in Ebling.

Yāsīn, Muḥammad Naʿīm. 'The End of Human Life in the Light of the Opinions of Muslim Scholars and Medical Findings' in I.O.M.S. (q.v.).

Zhorne, Jeff E., 'Organ Transplants: How Far Dare We Go?' in the *Plain Truth*. Cape Town: Ambassador College Agency (September 1985).

INDEX OF PROPER NAMES

GENERAL INDEX